WITHDRAWN

The Economic Surplus and
Neo-Marxism

The Economic Surplus and Neo-Marxism

Ron Stanfield
Idaho State University

Lexington Books
D.C. Heath and Company
Lexington, Massachusetts
Toronto   London

Library of Congress Cataloging in Publication Data

Stanfield, Ron.
    The economic surplus and neo-Marxism.

    Includes bibliographical references.
    1. United States—Economic conditions.
2. Capitalism.   3. Baran, Paul A. Monopoly capital.
I. Title.
HC106.S76   338.8'2'0973   73-951
ISBN 0-669-86736-5

Published simultaneously in Canada.

Printed in the United States of America.

International Standard Book Number: 0-669-86736-5

Library of Congress Catalog Card Number: 73-951

For Paul Sweezy And
The Memory of Paul Baran

Contents

List of Tables

Acknowledgments

The author wishes to acknowledge that, as is the case with human endeavor in general, this study is the product of the peculiar tension between cooperation and competition that is the life process. Robinson Crusoe could no more have penned this study than he could comprise a meaningful social and economic system.

Nomination is difficult. The study is a culmination of three years of graduate work at the University of Oklahoma, Norman, and there were many persons in the environment which conditioned the author's behavior.

Still, it would be remiss to make no attempt to acknowledge by name those who mean so much. The author has one consolation in undertaking this effort that must surely fail. That is that each comrade in cooperation and competition no doubt knows his influence on what follows more certainly than does the author.

Tom Curtis and Nelson Peach provided encouragement and direction throughout the research and penning of this book. They and John Piercey, John Munkirs, Don Kash, Jim Sturgeon, Ben Young, Ken Atwell, Arlene Bearman, Jack White, Joe Brown, Mike Ayers, Darius Conger, Andy Dane, Bob McMinn, and Andy Van Rest provided an environment in which only one quite dead could fail to learn. I was (am) not dead, and I learned much from them.

As is traditional but no less valid for being so, I reserve most credit for my friend and roommate of some years, Jacqueline.

December 15, 1972

1

The Economic Surplus

Statement of Purpose and Procedure

The main purpose of this study is to contribute to the body of literature known as neo-Marxism. The economic surplus concept lies at the heart of this literature. This study attempts to derive an operational definition of the economic surplus and to estimate its magnitude for the 1929-1970 period. This time series is then employed to evaluate the major work of neo-Marxism, *Monopoly Capital*.[1]

The procedure is to approach the economic surplus from the output side. The surplus is defined as the difference between potential output and essential consumption. Essential consumption is the sum of personal essential consumption and social essential consumption. Chapters 2 and 3 contain the conceptual foundations of these consumption elements. Chapters 4 and 5 are devoted to estimating their magnitudes for the 1929-1970 period.

Potential output is the output attainable if all factors of production were fully employed. In practice, it is the sum of actual output and some estimate of the gap or unutilized aggregate capacity. Chapter 6 contains the conceptual basis for the estimates of potential output set forth in Chapter 7.

Chapter 8 is the concluding chapter of the study. It contains, first, a composite summary of the procedures involved in earlier chapters. Second, three central hypotheses of neo-Marxism are evaluated in light of the evidence of the current study. Finally, such implications as are appropriate are drawn from the current study.

The evaluation of *Monopoly Capital* involves three hypotheses set forth by Baran and Sweezy. These are: one, that the economic surplus increases through time both absolutely and as a share of national income; two, that the share of the surplus seeking investment outlets increases through time; and three, that monopoly capitalism is incapable of absorbing this rising investment-seeking portion.

The first hypothesis, the rising surplus, is significant in Baran and Sweezy because they are concerned with the question of distributive income shares. The current study however, defines the surplus as the difference between potential output and essential output. In this context, the rising surplus signifies little more than the occurrence of technological change.

The second hypothesis, the rising investment-seeking portion of the surplus, is tested by, first, summing total essential consumption and nonessential personal consumption. Second, this sum is subtracted from potential output to approximate the investment-seeking portion of the surplus. The serial behavior of this sum relative to the surplus contradicts the Baran and Sweezy hypothesis.

The third hypothesis, the lack of sufficient absorption capacity, is equivalent to a downward trend in the operating rate of total capacity. This is tested by the serial ratios of actual to potential output. The lack of any insistent downward movement in this series contradicts the Baran and Sweezy hypothesis.

The fundamental theoretical point of the evaluation of *Monopoly Capital* is that Baran and Sweezy fail to sufficiently deny the applicability of the competitive law of value. They recognize rising selling costs and other phenomena that are inconsistent with competitive capitalism. However, they continue to equate labor income with necessary costs of production. Moreover, they regard all government expenditures as part of the surplus. Such treatment ignores the reality of a world characterized by big labor, big government, and big business. These repositories of power are not subject to the price system. Rather, they subject the price system to their own ends. Finally, a significant portion of essential consumption is governmentally supplied social consumption.

The Relevance of the Economic Surplus

The economic surplus is a derivative of Marx's concept of surplus value. Surplus value is the difference between the value produced by a worker in a given period and the share of that value necessary for the maintenance of the worker and the capital stock. Since, in a competitive situation, a commodity exchanges at its cost of production, the worker is paid only his cost of subsistence no matter that he produces in excess thereof.

The surplus concept central to neo-Marxism and the current study is related to that of surplus value. It is related because it emphasizes the difference between a given output and the cost of producing that output. However, it is not identical to surplus value because it does not assume that the competitive law of value is operative. That is, it is felt that the emergence of imperfect competition, trade unions, and an interventionist government have altered the face of capitalism and the nature of the surplus concept. The importance of this change is the theme of Chapter 8 of this study. To be very brief at this point, this evolution of capitalism necessitates the search for the surplus in terms of output rather than in terms of income.

The distinguishing characteristic of the surplus in neo-Marxist literature is therefore not its representation of surplus or unearned income shares. Rather, it is the element of social choice available as to the manner in which the surplus is to be employed.

The surplus of an economy in any given year represents the excess of potential total production over socially essential production in that year. . . . What basically distinguishes socially essential production from the surplus is that the former represents a first and largely unavoidable charge on the output of a society—without which it would begin to decay—whereas the latter is that part of its productive capacity that a society has some potential freedom to allocate among competing alternatives.[2]

Therefore, the question of income shares is interesting only to the degree that it affects the manner in which this social choice is made.

The surplus concept is fundamental in much of economic anthropology and economic history. It is used to explain the emergence of specialized labor and cities.[3]

In the prevailing explanation of the origin of social stratification and the emergence of full-time specialists ..., technological progress is pictured as leading to the production of economic surpluses. These are thought of as providing the biosocial precondition for the diversion of man-power from 'necessary' or 'subsistence' to specialized, culture-building activities. ...[4]

George Wilson employs the surplus concept to interpret economic history and the history of economic thought. That is, an interplay is found between the extant attitudes toward the surplus and its size and growth.[5] Weisskopf continues the passage quoted earlier by pointing out the extent to which the size and the use of its surplus determines the character of a society.

In a very significant sense, the nature of a society is revealed by the manner in which it disposes of its surplus. Societies are different to the extent that they make different choices about how to use [their resources]. But there is little choice to make about the provision of essential consumption. ... There is a real choice to make only about the use of the surplus. The surplus could be used to provide additional (nonessential) consumption for some or all the people; it could be used to invest in expanding the productive capacity of the economy; it could be used in fighting wars, in building palaces or churches; it could go unused if leisure were substituted voluntarily or involuntarily for the full use of productive capacity. In various parts of the world, and in various historical periods, different societies have been characterized by the different ways in which they have used their surplus.[6]

Thus, the surplus concept is also instrumental in the typification of economic systems. Historically, this question of the *form* of the economic surplus has been closely related to distributive shares. Thus, control of the surplus in feudal society is endowed in the income of the *rentier* as in early capitalism such control rests in the profits of capitalists. In a collectivized society, the surplus takes the form of a social fund to be administered by those who hold power in the extant institutional configuration. Of course, the existence of such a social fund is in itself not sufficient to assure democratic socialism. The fund may be administered by democratic or elitist or totalitarian decision-making. Here again the neo-Marxist must look beyond the nominal form of the surplus to its actual control and content.

Economic Surplus: Conceptually

The economic surplus concept to be used herein is very nearly that of Baran's "potential economic surplus." In fact, if Baran's original definition of potential economic surplus is taken to be his view, there is no significant difference involved.

> *Potential* economic surplus [is] the difference between the output that *could* be produced in a given natural and technological environment with the help of employable productive resources, and what might be regarded as essential consumption.
> This . . . refers to a different quantity of output than what would represent surplus value in Marx's sense. On the one hand, it *excludes* such elements of surplus as . . . *essential* consumption of capitalists, . . . *essential* outlays on government administration and the like; on the other hand, it comprises what is not covered by the concept of surplus value—the output lost in view of underemployment or misemployment of productive resources.[7]

The stipulation that reference is made to Baran's original definition is necessary inasmuch as he strays somewhat in the course of his argument, particularly in the confusing discussion of productive, unproductive, necessary, and unnecessary labor. Thus, scientists, physicians, artists, and teachers do "not fall under [Baran's] definition of unproductive labor." Yet, they are supported from the economic surplus. And this is supposed to make sense because, as Marx said, "Labor may be necessary without being productive."[8]

Quite probably the surplus concept Baran has in mind is the one found in a later work done in collaboration with Paul Sweezy. There, economic surplus is given an introductory "briefest possible definition [as] the difference between what a society produces and the costs of producing it."[9] If this is the case, then some of the services of scientists, artists, physicians, and teachers would appear to be costs of production. So also would a portion of government expenditures. For a portion of all these activities is necessary for the consumption of the population and for the static reproduction of the productive plant. For example, a portion of education expenditures is necessary to allow consumption at the socially judged minimal level and to reproduce the worker, i.e., his children, at his level of skill. Of course, a portion of educational services is investment, i.e., intended to enhance productive capacity rather than to merely reproduce it. And, of course, investment is properly considered an element of the economic surplus. Similarly for other expenditures, including those for health services and road construction, there arises a distinction between essential consumption and investment—not to mention waste and nonessential consumption, which are also to be observed.

As has been said, the economic surplus is defined herein as the difference between potential output and essential consumption (real costs of production). Potential output includes not only output actually attained but feasible output not attained due to unemployment and excess capacity. Essential consumption includes essential personal consumption and essential social consumption. Essential personal consumption is the aggregate quantity sufficient to provide the entire population with that level of consumption judged minimally adequate by society. Essential social consumption includes two elements, social overhead and capital consumption. Social overhead is the portion of government expenditures that is necessary to reproduce the existing productive capacity. Since essential personal consumption is a cost of production, this includes expenditures that are necessary parts of consumption or necessary to consume essential consumption. For example, the use and enjoyment of (not the earning of an income to buy) the minimal level might presuppose a certain educational level or a certain road network. Capital consumption is, of course, the "true" rate of wear and tear of capital resources. It is the amount of investment necessary to maintain the existing output capacity. This includes elements other than private investment. Public investment in roads and the like that are necessary for production and that experience wear and tear should also be depreciated. Similarly, a portion of educational expenses is for the replacement of manpower at existing skill levels. Finally, some allowance must be made for the social cost of natural resource depletion.

Economic Surplus: Empirically

Empirically, the procedure follows in a relatively straightforward fashion from the concept. This is not to deny, of course, the familiar compromise between conceptual precision and empirical practice. This compromise is probably somewhat more in evidence than is usual since the data available are cast in categories not altogether commensurate with those herein in question. Joseph Phillips stresses the data incommensurability problem especially in reference to the national income and product accounts collected by the Office of Business Economics of the U.S. Department of Commerce.[10] In this regard, the invisibility of sales effort expenditures and the unreliability of depreciation figures in these accounts are outstanding examples. The problem is certainly not absent in data from other sources. The personal consumption budget concept eventually adopted in the present study is prepared by the Bureau of Labor Statistics of the U.S. Department of Labor. Cast as it is in terms of market prices and income requirements, this budget includes elements that are not considered (essential) costs of production. These elements include such things as property incomes, government revenues, and selling costs that are embodied in market prices and must therefore be deleted.

It should be helpful at this point to compare the approach of the present study with that of the only other work known to this author that attempts to measure the economic surplus in systematic fashion. That is the work by Phillips mentioned above. Conceptually, Phillips is working on the base set down by Baran and Sweezy in the text of *Monopoly Capital*. He thus includes all government expenditures in the economic surplus, whereas in the current study some of these expenditures are treated as essential costs of production. Phillips is unable to incorporate meaningful estimates of two components of Baran and Sweezy's economic surplus, although some figures are presented to indicate their magnitude. One of these is the loss of output due to unemployment, which is included in the present study in tandem with excess capacity. The other is the penetration of the productive process by the sales effort in such phenomena as planned obsolescence. No attempt is made to incorporate this element into the present estimates. As in this study, Phillips relegates excess depreciation charges and an array of commercial and institutional costs to the economic surplus.[11]

The principal procedural difference between the present study and that of Phillips stems from the two sides of measuring aggregate economic activity. Phillips approaches estimation of the surplus from the income side. He totals property incomes, excess depreciation charges, government expenditures, and wastes in the business process to arrive directly at an estimate of the economic surplus. In the present study, the approach is more closely related to the output side of the ledger. Essential consumption, both personal and social, is estimated as the first step. Then, after estimating potential output, essential consumption is subtracted therefrom to arrive at an estimate of the economic surplus. And, most important of all, property incomes and government revenues are treated as transfer payments in the present study. This in effect means that they are eliminated from both potential output and essential consumption prior to the calculation of the surplus.

2

Definition of Personal Essential Consumption

In attempting to measure essential consumption, one is faced with a familiar problem dual. On the one hand, there is the difficulty of expressing the concept in a theoretically meaningful manner. On the other hand, there lies the inevitable compromise between theoretical substance and empirical (especially quantitative) substance. In this chapter and the next, the essential consumption concept is derived and given quantifiable expression. In Chapters 4 and 5, serial statistics are presented estimating the magnitude of essential consumption for the period 1929-1970.

Conceptual Budgets

Subsistence Minimum

There are a variety of concepts that come to mind in association with the term (personal) essential consumption. Probably the most common is that of the subsistence minimum that permeates all of classical economics. The subsistence minimum in classical economic science is the "natural" or long-run normal price (or wage) for labor under competitive conditions. In a famous passage, Ricardo shows the social content of the concept by defining it as:

... that price which is necessary to enable the labourers ... to subsist and to perpetuate their race, without either increase or diminution.[1]

Similarly, Marx spoke of subsistence as the "value of labour power," which is the

... labour-time necessary for the production and ... reproduction [of a given labour-power that has] ... a definite quantity of the average labour of society incorporated in it. Labour-power exists only as a capacity, or power of the living individual. Its production ... presupposes his existence. [Hence,] the production of labour-power consists in [the] reproduction ... or maintenance [of the individual labourer]. For his maintenance he requires a given quantity of the means of subsistence ... the value of labour-power is the value of the means necessary for the maintenance of the labourer.[2]

The subsistence minimum wage is then the wage that will barely allow or induce the laborer to maintain himself and his family. If the actual wage is sufficiently below this minimum, the worker and his family may starve and become susceptible to disease. Short of this, the wage may be insufficient to allow the worker to marry and reproduce himself, which of course implies a distinction between a wage allowing only physiological existence and a wage providing inducement to procreate.

This distinction rests wholly on the relativity of the subsistence minimum. As Ricardo observes, the necessary subsistence minimum includes "those comforts which custom renders absolute necessaries," i.e., "the natural rate of wages" affords "moderate comforts."[3] And, says Ricardo:

It is not to be understood that the natural price of labour, estimated even in food and necessaries is absolutely fixed and constant. It varies at different times in the same country, and very materially differs in different countries. It essentially depends on the habits and customs of the people.[4]

Marx is even more explicit,

... the number and extent of [the laborer's] so-called necessary wants, as also the modes of satisfying them, are themselves the product of historical development, and depend therefore to a great extent on the degree of civilisation of a country, more particularly on the conditions under which, and consequently on the habits and degree of comfort in which, the class of free labourers has been formed. [Contrary] to the case of other commodities, there enters into the determination of the value of labour-power a historical and moral element.[5]

Thus, in the words of Baran, the

... wants of people are complex historical phenomena reflecting the dialectic interaction of their physiological requirements on the one hand, and the prevailing social and economic order on the other.[6]

Yet, it should be noted that this historical and cultural relativity of the subsistence minimum need not rob the concept of substance. As both Marx and Baran are quick to point out, despite this lack of temporal or spatial fixity,

... in a given country, at a given period, the average quantity of the means of subsistence necessary for the labourer is practically known.[7]

And, whether living standards are in general low or high, it is possible to make

... a judgment on the amount and composition of real income necessary for what is socially considered to be [a] decent livelihood.[8]

Other Minimum Consumption Concepts

Other concepts of minimum consumption standards or levels,[9] such as those defining minimum quantities for efficiency or for health and decency or those defining the poverty line, either add nothing to the classical subsistence standard for present purposes or are special cases thereof in the broad, relative interpretation accepted herein. An efficiency standard represents a quantity of consumption that a family group must have if its members are to function as productive and useful members of society.[10] The appeal of such a standard is the presumption that it can be set by objective, "hard" scientific judgment rather than by social or ethical values.[11] A strong case can be made for such a standard *vis-à-vis* underdeveloped countries, since large segments of the populace in such countries hover around physical subsistence levels.[12] However, such a standard in this case is a special case of the classical subsistence standard. The "degree of civilization" (read economic process) is simply not high enough to support significant relative or psychological factors for more than a small fraction of the population. Moreover, such a standard neglects a high degree of interaction between the standard of consumption and the nature of the efficiency in question. That is, the question "Efficient for what?" is in part determined by the standard or level of consumption.[13] Further, relative considerations inevitably enter the picture to some degree, as when efficiency is lowered by a feeling on the part of workers that their tools or consumption levels are inferior to those elsewhere.[14]

Consumption standards pertaining to the minimum consumption level necessary to maintain a family in "health and decency" possess even less claim to conceptual separability. Begging the question as to the possibility of setting nonrelative standards for health, there seems to be little doubt that "decency" is a thoroughly relative concept, imbedded as it must be in the moral sensibilities of society. And, given this relativity, there remains no ground upon which to demand conceptual distinction from the classical standard as interpreted herein.

Most of the comments made concerning the above two standards apply with equal force to standards defining the "poverty line." From the ongoing debate concerning relative and absolute poverty, it seems clear that relative poverty is simply more relative than absolute poverty, the latter being relative to some degree. Ethical and social judgments concerning the relation of the individual to society and *vice versa* remain a large element in determining what poverty is. Still, present purposes aside, there is some justification for separating the poverty standard from the classical subsistence standard. The former relates mainly to those employed or lowly employed and the latter to those normally or averagely employed. Hence, for many purposes such as dealing with the social problem of the lowly or nonemployable, the poverty standard has relevance. Present purposes considered, however, the poverty standard has little to offer.

Finally, no systematic treatment of so-called "maintenance" standards is necessary. Such standards obviously beg the question "What is to be maintained?" To answer the question with substance is to reply subsistence, efficiency, health and decency, or kindred concepts.

Empirical Budgets

Investigations aimed at establishing minimum necessary quantity or cost budgets have progressed in relation to economic development. Helen Lamale notes that before 1860, there was little or no interest in measuring income adequacy or in the budgets necessary to determine such adequacy.[15] In the forty years after 1860, interest in budget standards arose and emphasized physical subsistence minimums. These budgets were based on consumer surveys of families with minimum incomes.

By the turn of the century, two influences had begun to influence budget studies. First, scientific knowledge had sufficiently progressed to allow stipulation of minimum necessary quantities for food and later for housing. The initial impact of this was the shift to so-called "ideal" budget standards, which were set without recourse to actual consumer expenditure surveys. In such budgets, the intent was to determine minimum consumption levels on purely "hard" scientific fundamentals. With the general growth of wealth in the United States, however, a second influence developed: the explicit inclusion of a social or psychological factor in minimum budgets. Thus, in the three decades prior to the Great Depression, there were developed numerous budgets designed to quantify "health and decency," "fair American," or "minimum comfort" budgets.[16] After a minor setback in the Depression, this "social" conception of budgets gained and has held full sway. The fusion of the "ideal" or scientific standards and the empirical consumer expenditure surveys has been the common methodology in the post-World War II period.[17]

Generally, these empirical studies, which set out to provide quantity and/or cost budgets, do not intend to correspond with the conceptual standards discussed above. The empirical budgets are frequently motivated by a particular social or political purpose rather than by theoretical curiosity. Quantitative budget types have been widely used in measuring costs of living and its changes and in aiding in the determination of wage and welfare levels. The budgets reviewed below are limited to those of the United States after 1929.[18] Further, the discussion here is limited to definition of the standard of consumption contents of these budgets. Serial data on quantities and costs are presented as needed in Chapter 4.

WPA Maintenance Budget

The Works Progress Administration's "maintenance" budget is for an "unskilled manual worker's" family consisting of the husband, wife, a son age thirteen, and a daughter age eight.[19] This budget "provides not only for physical needs but also gives some consideration to psychological values." The budget provides for an "adequate diet at minimum cost," as defined by the Bureau of Home

Economics, and a four- or five-room house or apartment in "at least a fair state of repair [with a private] indoor bath and toilet." Clothing and household furnishings are provided "with some regard for social as well as material needs." Numerous miscellaneous expenses such as carfare, "simple leisure time activities," gas, ice, electricity, and a daily newspaper are included in the budget. The budget is described as being not so liberal as a "health and decency" budget, but providing more than a "minimum of subsistence" living. Further, it is said that the maintenance budget does not approach "a satisfactory American standard of living" in that such a standard would include "an automobile, better housing and equipment, a more varied diet, and preventive medical care [as well as] provision, . . for future education of children and for economic security through saving."[20]

BLS City Workers' Family Budget

The longest serially running budget is the City Workers' Family Budget (CWFB) prepared by the Bureau of Labor Statistics for a city worker's family of four (husband, age thirty-eight; wife, age thirty-six; son, age thirteen; and daughter, age eight). The original CWFB for 1946-1947 is described as being neither a "subsistence" nor a "luxury" budget, but a "modest but adequate" one. It was designed to estimate

. . . the dollar cost required to maintain [the specified] family at a level of adequate living—to satisfy prevailing standards of what is necessary for health, efficiency, the nurture of children, and for participation in community activities.[21]

The budget represents scientific standards of adequacy in areas such as food, housing, and medical care, modified within acceptable adequate ranges by actual consumer expenditures. The budget was prepared with the assistance of the Bureau of Human Nutrition and Home Economics of the U.S. Department of Agriculture and the Bureau of Research and Statistics of the Social Security Administration, according to standards set by the National Research Council's Food and Nutrition Board, the American Public Health Association's Committee on the Hygiene of Housing, and the Federal Public Housing Administration. Data on consumer expenditures collected in the period 1929-1941 and checked in 1944 were used to determine the content of the budget within the accepted range.[22]

The Bureau of Labor Statistics discontinued pricing the original CWFB in October, 1951, since the quantities and qualities of goods and services therein were based on standards prevailing prior to 1941. An interim CWFB was published in 1960 which revised the content of the original budget to reflect the level of living prevalent in the 1950s. The interim budget did not involve a revision of the modest but adequate concept nor of the type, size, or composition of the representative family. The same agencies as before advised as to the scientific standards for food and housing, and the method for choosing specified goods meeting these standards remained that of surveying actual consumer expenditures. And, as before, these expenditure patterns were used to determine quantities where scientific standards were not available. The primary consumer expenditure data used were from the 1950 Bureau of Labor Statistics study. The BLS estimated that of the 40 percent increase in the cost of the budget between 1951 and 1959, more than half reflected rising living standards, the rest being due to rising prices.[23]

A more complete revision of the CWFB was published in 1967. Again, no change was made in the basic "modest but adequate" concept, in the representative family composition, nor in the method of combining scientific standards and consumer expenditure patterns. The revised budget was meant to reflect norms of living extant in the 1960s, and expenditure studies of 1961-1962 were used. One change in format was the inclusion of small towns, apparently those adjacent to the thirty-nine major metropolitan areas. This being the case, no substantial inconsistency with earlier budgets is expected since the earlier budgets included suburban areas. Other changes reflect rising living standards. Homeowner costs such as mortgage principal and interest payments, insurance, taxes, and maintenance costs were added. A higher percentage of families was assumed to own automobiles, more meals away from home were included, and meals at home were based entirely on the U.S. Department of Agriculture adequate diet at moderate cost plan rather than an average of the low and moderate cost plans as in the past. No estimate of the percentage of the total cost increase due to higher living standards is given.[24] Since 1967, the CWFB has been priced at three levels with the intermediate level corresponding to the "modest but adequate" concept.[25]

Social Security Administration
Near-Poverty Line Budget

Of relatively recent origin are the poverty line budgets assembled by the Social Security Administration's Division of Research and Statistics. Of interest here is the "near-poverty" budget which is based upon the United States Department of Agriculture's adequate diet at minimum cost "low-cost" plan rather than the "poverty budget" based upon the USDA's "economy" food plan. The latter is 75 percent to 80 percent of the basic low-cost plan. The method used by Ms. Orshansky in deriving the poverty line is to estimate from consumer surveys the proportion of income going to food, then to use this proportion and the cost of the low-cost food budget to estimate the total budget necessary for families of various sizes and compositions.[26]

The provisions of this budget are rather stringent. The skill at household management required to stretch the budget to attain the adequate food seems to be extraordinary. At the low-cost level, 90 cents per day per person in 1963 prices is allowed for food. There is no provision in the budget for meals away from home nor even milk or coffee to supplement a brown-bag lunch.[27]

Although the Social Security Administration budget shares some characteristics with the Bureau of Labor Statistics budget, most notably the methodological fusion of scientific and social judgment, it is clearly less suited than the BLS budget for present purposes. Primarily, this is due to the conceptual difference involved, although the wider scope of data collection by the BLS is also a compelling factor. The SSA budget does not reflect social judgment as to what is "normal" or "standard." It is a minimum for aberrant people, not for the mainstream even of manual labor's society. It is for the *lumpenproletariat* perhaps, but not for the proletariat. It is a stopgap budget to provide enough in the short run to enable a long-run answer to be developed for a pressing social problem. It cannot be accepted as the essential standard of consumption for a nation so opulent as the United States.

Selection of the BLS Budget

The Bureau of Labor Statistics City Workers' Family Budget, i.e., the "modest but adequate" standard of living budget, is the budget concept to be used for personal essential consumption. Aside from the convenience involved in its availability and its methodological scope, this budget seems to reflect the spirit of the subsistence minimum as defined in the writings of Ricardo, Marx, and Baran, if allowance is made for the degree of civilization of the United States. Provision for an adequate standard of living seems reasonable in light of the wealth of the United States. The budget meets the test of objectivity in both aspects of the BLS methodology. On the other hand, the budget provisions for food and housing meet available scientific criteria for adequacy. On the other hand, inasmuch as the content of the budget is based as well on actual consumer expenditures, it reflects prevailing social judgment as to the customary levels of adequacy.

If anything, the budget may be considered too liberal in its provisions since it is ostensibly more than a minimum subsistence standard of living. However, if subsistence is given the broader, relative interpretation as it is herein, this objection seems invalid. There is ample evidence that the budget is intended to reflect a minimum budget in terms of prevailing social judgment.

The budget was designed to represent the estimated dollar cost required to maintain [the specified] family at a level of adequate living—to satisfy prevailing standards of what is necessary. . . . [28]

[The budget represents] the annual cost of a worker's family budget which includes the kinds and quantities of necessary goods and services, according to standards prevailing in the large cities of the U.S.[29]

[The intention of the budget is to measure] the cost at current prices in large cities of family living which [meet] American standards of what is required.

The budget therefore should represent the necessary minimum with respect to items included and their quantities as determined by prevailing standards of what is needed for health, efficiency, nurture of children, social participation, and the maintenance of self-respect and the respect of others.[30]

Although the level of living represented by the budget cannot be briefly described by words having scientific precision yet, the concept of a necessary minimum is a reality. Judgment is constantly being expressed as to what is necessary. . . . When it is said that the budget recommended is intended to cover the necessary minimum, 'necessary' is to be given the common interpretation as including what will meet the conventional and social as well as biological needs. It represents what men commonly expect to enjoy, feel that they have lost status and are experiencing deprivation if they cannot enjoy, and what they insist upon having. Such a budget is not an absolute and unchanging thing. The prevailing judgment of the necessary will vary with the changing values of the community, with the advance of scientific knowledge of human needs, with the advance of scientific knowledge of human needs, with the productive power of the community and therefore what people commonly enjoy and see others enjoy.[31]

3

Definition of Social Essential Consumption

General Social Overhead

Social Balance

Conceptually, the magnitude of public goods and services to be considered general social overhead is that which represents essential costs of production. This implies essence in two ways. First, the public expenditure in question must be necessary in the sense of being a socially necessary cost of production for a given level of consumption. Second, the given level of consumption must itself be necessary in the sense of just maintaining the current productive capacity. That is, to be essential, a government expenditure must represent not simply a necessary adjunct to private consumption, but a necessary adjunct to essential private consumption.

John Kenneth Galbraith effectively demonstrates that there is some more or less definite level of public production (read consumption) which is a requisite complement to a given level of private production (read consumption).[1] Essentially, Galbraith extends the older conception of complementarity, balance, or proportionality of production in different production compartments[2] to include production in the public sphere. This complementarity can be direct, as when the operation of a given quantity of motor vehicles necessitates a certain road and traffic regulation network. Or, it can be more subtle, as when a given style of living, including a certain mode of production and degrees of leisure or mobility, necessitates certain levels of education, maintenance of order, and other social services.

Galbraith is concerned with showing that a general complementary relation exists. Hence, such specific examples as he notes are just that, examples to demonstrate his general principle. Moreover, he is concerned with the necessary public complements to private consumption in general and does not seek to differentiate essential and nonessential consumption. His examples thus lack the thoroughness and characteristics necessary to be of service for current purposes, notwithstanding the importance of his general principle of social balance.

Functions of the State in Economic Theory

Classical Theory

Before meeting directly the problems involved in the present concept of social overhead consumption, it is necessary to digress momentarily to review the

15

functions of the state in the history of economic theory. A convenient and impregnably defensible starting point for such a review is classical economics and Adam Smith. Smith states that there exist four areas in which government expenditure is necessary.[3] The first three are the basic functions of government: defense of the sovereign territory, maintenance of a system of internal order and justice, and provision of such public works and institutions that cannot be profitably undertaken by the private sector. The fourth necessary expense, upholding the dignity of the sovereign, is not a function in Smith's view but is nevertheless necessary.

The expenditures related to defense, order, and the dignity of the government are relatively specific and straightforward and require no discussion. Smith's third basic function is less direct, containing the subfunctions of facilitation of commerce and education of the populace. Under the facilitation of commerce, Smith subsumes a variety of specific activities: construction and maintenance of roads, bridges, canals, and harbors; operation of monetary and postal systems; and the "protection of trade in general" by maintaining international relations and customs agencies. Education of the people includes public education for the children of the common classes and the "chiefly" religious instruction of people of all ages.

The most important characteristic of Smith's view of the public function is not any set of the specific activities he mentions, but the potential malleability of his basic functions. This is especially true of the third function of providing

... those public institutions and those public works, which, though they may be in the highest degree advantageous to a great society, are, however, of such a nature, that the profit could never repay the expence to any individual or small number of individuals, and which it therefore cannot be expected that any individual or small number of individuals should erect or maintain.[4]

Although Smith may have had some more or less definite minimal set of activities in mind, his statement in general terms is open to broad interpretation should a need for such arise.[a]

This was sensed by the younger Mill. He notes the two common necessary government interventions given in abstract treatises, protection from force and fraud, then lists several others to demonstrate the overly restrictive nature of the abstract intervention classes.[5] After enumerating such common and unobjectionable governmental activities as administration of property, record keeping, enforcement of contracts, providing care for the irresponsible, coining money, maintaining roads, and prescribing standards of weight and measure, Mill conjectures that the list might be expanded indefinitely. He concludes that not

[a]As is shown in the discussion of modern theory, the modern camp is of two lineages from Smith. The libertarian tradition clings to Smith's specificity and his view of the government as a necessary evil to be minimized. The modern liberal school of thought emphasizes Smith's general principle of intervention where the market fails.

only is it impossible to draw a definitive list for government functions through time and space, but also that no general principle is possible save that of expedience.

The classicists clearly held some type of minimum theory in regard to the functions of government. The most generally held interpretation of this minimum is that the classicists were convinced of the theoretical adequacy of the natural order concept and the efficacy of *laissez-faire* economic policy. This is the root of divergence between the two great sides of modern economic thought: the libertarian tradition that embraces *laissez-faire* and views government as a necessary evil to be minimized, and the modern liberal tradition which grants a greater role to government in providing the necessary institutional setting for social optimization.

The other possible interpretation is that the classicists' minimum government function view corresponds to their subsistence, necessary costs of production view of private production. This interpretation would have it that Smith sought to define the long-run minimally adequate functions that the government must provide. Whether or not this is a valid interpretation of the classicists' views of the role of government, it is similar to the concept that is sought in the present study.

Modern Theory

Neoclassical economic thought is largely devoid of systematic treatment of the government's role in society. Thus, the seminal and colossal work of neoclassicism, Marshall's *Principles of Economics*, contains only scattered references to government functions such as the undertaking of large risks and the provision of education, health, and sanitation services.[6] Similarly, Pigou, in his *A Study in Public Finance* devotes only a very few pages to the question of government spending, concerning himself primarily with considerations of taxation.[7]

Despite this lack of direct treatment, neoclassicism does contain important elements for the development of the theory of government functions. On the one hand, these elements surround Marshall's tax-bounty analysis, as later reformulated by Pigou and refined by Lerner in the terminology of social and private benefits and costs. On the other hand, implications for the government's role flow from Marshall's treatment of external economies and the anomaly of decreasing cost industries under perfect competition, as later developed into theories of alternative competitive structures by Sraffa, Robinson, and Chamberlin.[8] These two areas of thought thoroughly undermined the microeconomic basis of the vulgar *laissez-faire Harmonielehre*, and replaced it in actual if not theoretical practice with a more or less active role for government in maintaining the appropriate institutional setting.

In combination with the repudiation of Say's Law, the macroeconomic

Harmonielehre, by the Keynesian Revolution, these developments forced a schism in the classical liberalism camp. On the one side of this cleavage of chronologically modern thought is the conservative, libertarian tradition closely associated with the "Chicago School." This strand of opinion continues the interpretation of the classical minimum government functions as being the minimization of a necessary evil. Thus, Milton Friedman, in listing the functions of government consonant with its "role in a free society," largely reiterates the list of *specific* functions provided by Adam Smith.[9]

On the other side of modern thought, modern liberalism, is to be found the *general* formulation of Smith on the government's role following the line of Mill's expediency principle. This strand of opinion, which has come to dominate the ideology and economics of the corporate state, unanimously assumes the posture of providing *justification* for various public functions or *interventions*.

As such, all of these approaches either flow into or out of Richard A. Musgrave's classic trichotomy of the government's functions into allocative, distributive, or stabilization interventions.[10] Thus, the government intervenes to secure adjustments in the pattern of resource allocation that are made necessary or desirable by market imperfections, decreasing production costs, externalities, divergences between public and private risk or time preferences, social wants, or merit wants.[b] Again, the government intervenes to secure adjustments in the pattern of income distribution to accord such distribution with social consensus as to equity and efficiency. Finally, the government intervenes to secure adjustments in the aggregate level of economic activity in order to sustain the neo-Keynesian macroeconomic trilogy of high employment, high economic growth, and relatively stable wage and price levels.

Musgrave's justly famous multiple theory of budget determination is important not so much for adding any specific functions to the governmental realm—his examples are all well known to the readers of Smith, Pigou, Keynes, and Lerner—but for his assimilation and theoretical refinement of that which went before and for the elasticity of his constructs for that which follow him. His precise articulation and classification of the justifications for intervening with the political ballot box to adjust the solution of the economic ballot box, or to provide a solution when the market affords none, lend an air of dignity and legitimacy in the troubled atmosphere of public activity in a society of predominantly *laissez-faire* mentality. The nomenclature of social wants wherein the exclusion principle is inoperative, or of merit wants wherein the market is overly or underly stingy, is far more elegant than Smith's lack of profit motivations for individuals or Lerner's cumbersome equations of marginal private and social costs.

Moreover, in his elegance, Musgrave provides a quantum leap in generality. His schema are sufficiently abstract to be stretched to encompass an indefinitely

---

[b]Musgrave's formulation could no doubt be improved by recognition of externalities in general as being involved in all his intervention cases; but this is not of relevance here.

wide range of activities into the government sphere. For example, it is conceptually valid that the government do anything under the proviso of the highly elastic merit want principle; all that is necessary is that empirical evidence be presented that social consensus affords a positive or negative value on some good or service beyond the valuation given by the market mechanism. And, in contrast to the compromising mood of Mill's expediency principle, all this is accomplished without sacrificing the dignified aura of precision and legitimacy.

Thus, the contemporary *Zeitgeist* as to the state's role is thoroughly transformed. A clearer example of ideological adjustment to the objective socio-historical conditions is difficult to find.[11]

Marxist Theory

It remains but to survey the Marxist theory of the state before stock can be taken as to the instrumentality of this digression for present purposes. This survey is of necessity brief because the Marxists have largely neglected government functions in general for one particular government function. The Marxist theory of the state derives fundamentally from Engel's work on the origin of the state. That is, with the breakdown of primitive, classless communism and the rise of class society, antagonisms arose between the various classes. Thus, historical forces were created which produced the state as an instrument to moderate these class antagonisms.[12]

Corollary to this theorem of its origin, the state is seen as the executive arm of the ruling class. This sharply differentiates the Marxist theory of the state as power broker from the "bourgeois" theory of the state as a more or less neutral mechanism for resolving conflicts of interests within society. Thus, the state in Marxist theory is not a neutral, exogenous social force, but an instrument of class struggle internal to the model of social processes.[13]

This said, there is little that remains of the Marxist theory of the state insofar as the functions of government are concerned. In driving home the point that the state is an instrument of class struggle, Marxist thought largely ignores the state functions that are necessary costs of production more or less independent of the class struggle. Independence does not, of course, deny interaction of social consumption and class struggle. For, albeit that the existent set of class relations influences the quantity and quality of social essential consumption, the point is that, however variable, such consumption exists.

It is curious that writers so convinced of the necessity of socialism neglect the necessity of social consumption. Thus, one reads *Capital* to find the state largely reduced to the arena of struggle for shorter work hours or other industrial relations legislation.[14] Nor are correctives to be found in modern Marxist thought, orthodox or revisionist. John Strachey analyzes the state largely in terms of its being an arena in which is waged a popular, representative struggle for higher wages and job security.[15] Ralph Miliband focuses largely on the class politics of controlling opinion and policy.[16] This approach is not altered by Paul Sweezy in his classic restatement of Marxist economic theory,[17] nor in the recent reformulation thereof in collaboration with Paul Baran.[18] It is especially instructive to compare Baran's analysis of the state, cast completely in familiar class struggle terms, with his statement concerning essential consumption, where he explicitly refers to "*essential* outlays on government administration and the like."[19]

None of this is meant, of course, to deprecate the work of these authors, nor the importance of the class struggle aspects of the state in society. Rather, the point is that in a body of literature so enamored with necessary social costs of production and the economic surplus in excess thereof, one expects, indeed must demand, that attention be given to costs of production that arise in the public sector.

General Social Overhead in this Study

The above review of literature should make it obvious to the reader that it is of little direct help for the present purpose of defining and measuring essential government functions. None of this literature is oriented toward the social overhead concept as here envisioned. Yet this concept is an indispensable component of costs of production viewed as consumption just adequate to maintain extant productive capacity. Thus, the necessary course of action is to develop afresh such a concept and a mode of estimating its magnitude.

Conceptual and Empirical Problems

A proper starting point for this task is to survey the problems to be encountered in fulfilling it. These problems may be explicated by contrasting the measurement of social consumption with that of personal consumption. In the latter area, there is a well-established conceptual and empirical base—most notably the Bureau of Labor Statistics series. The City Workers' Family Budget is based upon two sources of information: scientific and social judgments as to necessity or minimum adequacy.

In the social consumption area, there is, first, no established scientific bases as to necessity. It is doubtful that information is plausible for social consumption that would correspond to the "hard" scientific or physiological standards available for food consumption, except possibly in matters of public health.

Second, it is not possible to use prevailing social judgment directly to determine minimally adequate levels of social consumption. One difficulty in this regard is enumerating objective criteria for ascertaining social judgment on such matters. There is no clearcut measure of choice in the political system that corresponds to the decisions expressed in the market. Consensus of collective opinion is not so easily measured as is the sum of individual private opinions on a particular good or service.

But this problem is not insurmountable. Actual levels of legislative appropriations are measurable and could be taken to represent prevailing consensus in the absence of adequate, direct popular opinion surveys. This involves overlooking the imperfections of political mechanisms and substituting a level for a standard, but could be used so long as these limitations were expressed.

A second difficulty is not so tractable. For the most part, social judgment as expressed in consumer expenditure surveys involves opinions as to magnitudes of *current* consumption. By contrast, many public goods and services involve substantial degrees of future orientation. That is, they assume the character of investment in that they are to enhance the quality of the future.

This distinction is not absolute. Some private consumption expenditures are future oriented by subjective intent and/or objective results. Thus, Theodore Schultz views private expenditures on education, health, migration, and even food and shelter, as significant investment elements.[20] Schultz is not using investment in the present sense of that which increases productive capacity. Otherwise, he surely would not have viewed the level of food consumption, a maintenance cost, as investment.[21] Clearly, qualitative or quantitative improvements in food may be investment, but not a static level of food. The distinction being made is, of course, that our concern presently focuses on what is commonly called *net* investment whereas Schultz seems to have reference to *gross* investment.

No doubt there are net investment elements in private consumption expenditures. However, the City Workers' Family Budget is rather stringent on such items. For example, the moderate standard budget for spring 1967 contains a provision of $55.50 for school and college expenses, including "books, supplies, tuition, fees, etc."[22] It thus seems a minor limitation to proceed without the consumption/investment distinction in the private sector, although retaining it is a necessary element in the public sector.

Procedure

The estimating procedure for essential public expenditures must then take the level of such expenditures as a standard and adjust this magnitude according to the consumption/investment distinction. Not all government expenditures are subject to this distinction. Some represent *in toto*, or very nearly so, current social consumption. For example, expenditures for general government administration and civilian safety are essentially "used up" in the current period. Some other expenditures, notably transfer payments and defense expenditures, are neither essential consumption nor investment. Still others, such as research and development financing, are to be regarded as purely investment. Thus, the consumption/investment distinction does not come into play in cases involving pure consumption, essential or nonessential, or pure investment.

Only for the remainder of public expenditures, primarily in the areas of health, education, and public works, is the consumption/investment distinction relevant. In all these cases, estimation is hampered due to the lack of a capital budget for the public sector. Hence, it would be exceedingly difficult to approach the problem directly and attempt to differentiate government expenditures by their character, that is, to differentiate between expenditures that are to provide current services and expenditures on buildings and the like that yield services through time.

Thus, the problem is here approached from the output side. In the case of roads and public utilities, proportionality is assumed to exist between their necessary level and the level of total output. Therefore, ratios measuring the change in GNP through time are used to assign expenditures in these areas to consumption and investment. In the case of education, ratios measuring changes in the size and level of educational attainment of the labor force are used to make this assignment. Finally, in the case of expenditures for health and hospital services, ratios indicating changes in the level of hospital use are employed to make the assignment.

Capital Consumption

The second element of essential social consumption is capital consumption. Conceptually, capital consumption is straightforward. It is the decrease of usefulness incurred by the productive plant through use and the passage of time. In annual terms, it is the amount of the capital stock used up or consumed in production during the year.

> For instance, if a . . . machine lasts for 10 years, it is plain that during that working period its total value is gradually transferred to the product of the 10 years.
> As regards the means of production, what is really consumed is their use-value. . . .[23]

Further, although the eventual useful life of an individual piece of capital cannot be known in advance, its *expected* useful life can be known. For just as the impossibility of predicting the life span of individual human beings does not prevent the use of actuarial principles,

> So it is with the instruments of labour. It is known by experience how long on the average a machine of a particular kind will last.[24]

Capital Consumption in Contemporary Capitalism

However, upon a change in focus to the search for an empirically operational definition of capital consumption in contemporary capitalism, one encounters a severe loss of the directness characteristic of the concept in the abstract. First of all, the prominence of technological change causes obsolescence and replacement of capital goods prior to the end of their useful life. This creates a conflict between pure durability, the retention of capacity for productive use, and technological durability, the capacity for efficient productive use relative to alternative capital.

Nor is obsolescence a simple concept. To the contrary, as Royall Brandis demonstrates, there are not only a variety of forms of technological obsolescence, but also several forms of purely social and economic obsolescence.[25] The latter are instances wherein a capital good "wears out" due to such things as demand shifts or demographic changes, not because it is less efficient than an alternative, but because a decline in the need for its output occurs.

It is not at all clear whether the criterion for delineating the useful lifetime of a capital good is physical durability, technological durability, or economic durability. Indeed, the question probably revolves entirely around the circumstances of analysis. Thus, if the analysis concerns business behavior, that psychological wasteland, economic or even financial lifetimes may be entirely appropriate.

It is clear, however, that much economic obsolescence could be avoided via improved social planning. This follows largely from the fact that production carried out under a rational plan would practically solve the disproportionality problem. Capacity would be established sectorally and geographically in coordination with the socially planned budget, not according to the profit expectations of a myriad of independent decision-makers. Thus, the phenomenon noted by Steindl of capacity expansion in the face of declining utilization of capacity and other forms of "competitive waste" would be avoided.[26] Economic obsolescence is therefore properly considered a surplus element in the current context.

Under a rationally planned system, technological obsolescence could be increased or decreased. The rational planning of scientific and technological development and implementation involves social judgments on a variety of factors that are not knowable *a priori*. However, from the vantage point of essential capital consumption, technological obsolescence must be viewed as capacity-increasing investment and be therefore excluded from necessary costs of production. Thus, in the current paper, the view of Frankel that a capital good's "durability" or physical life is appropriate for depreciation purposes is accepted.[27]

This conceptual acceptance done, however, the problems caused by the various types of obsolescence are not completely removed. For economic and technological obsolescence, to the extent that they precede physical obsolescence, deny the experience upon which Marx depended for the determination of the average useful lifetimes of capital goods.[28] In short, if usable machines are replaced after ten years of use, there is no basis of repeated experience for ascertaining whether their physical lifetimes number eleven, twenty, or thirty years.

There are additional problems encountered in the accounting practices embodied in the aggregate capital consumption estimates made by the Office of Business Economics. In his attempt to measure "real depreciation in the USA," the Soviet economist Golanskii emphasizes the infamous productive/unproductive distinction:

... American statistics, ignoring the distinction between productive and unproductive spheres, include in depreciation of fixed capital the wear and tear on dwellings and other buildings and property which do not participate in production.[29]

This distinction between productive and unproductive capital is, of course, not employed in the current paper. Instead, costs of production herein involve the essential/nonessential distinction. Thus, for example, depreciation on dwellings is at least in part a cost of production.

This leads to the question as to the necessity of various fixed capital. No direct attempt is made to delete depreciation on nonessential capital stock. Rather, the deletion is made indirectly when the essential consumption estimates are adjusted for surplus elements in market prices. Thus, the costs of production in such areas as advertising, public relations, and finance are to be deleted from essential consumption. Moreover, depreciation charges in such areas are relatively low owing to their labor intensive nature.

Other problems related to current accounting practices are the use of original cost rather than replacement cost, the distortion of the time distribution of depreciation by legal changes, the inclusion of some capital expenditures in current expenses, and the lack of a capital budget in the public sector.[30] The overall effect of these problems must surely be toward an overstatement of depreciation for a given year.[31] The only one tending toward understatement is the use of original cost in a period of upward price movement. Aside from the theoretical issue of whether original or replacement cost is the proper point of concern,[32] the magnitude of this effect is surely offset by the tendencies toward overstatement. The treatment of price and tax law changes is clarified in the procedural discussion immediately below, and the problem of the government's capital budget is waived. As for capital outlays charged to current expense, the Office of Business Economics estimates such outlays and their depreciation for equipment with a life expectancy in excess of one year and for certain exploration expenses associated with natural resources exploitation. Hence, the problem is here neglected as being relatively insignificant.

Procedure for Estimating Essential Capital Consumption

The procedure adopted to estimate capital consumption concentrates mainly on avoiding the distortion caused by legal changes. The method and data provided by Allan H. Young[33] are used. Young uses several alternative methods for estimating depreciation. The one used here is designated "historical cost, straight line, F service lives." "Historical cost" refers to original cost and "straight line" to one of several accounting methods for the treatment of depreciation. The term "F service lives" refers to the schedule of service lives of capital goods, as periodically published by the Internal Revenue Service. For all years, the one used by Young for the description in question is the revised edition of 1942.[34]

Young's data include only nonfinancial corporations, omitting other businesses and residential structures. Therefore, to get figures relevant to the current study, his figures for nonfinancial, corporate depreciation are first divided by the Office of Business Economics' nonfinancial corporate depreciation figures. Then, this ratio is applied to the total depreciation figures of the Office of Business Economics to estimate the relevant depreciation figures.

This procedure is subject to several limitations. For one, there is evidence that the Bulletin F service lives are somewhat less than actual service lives—although there is also contrary evidence.[35] Moreover, due to technological and economic obsolescence, actual service lives may be assumed to fall short of physical service lives, the concept deemed appropriate herein. Also, it may be expected that the service lives of residential structures are greater than those for corporate capital goods. To offset these overstatement tendencies to some degree, original cost rather than replacement cost figures are used. Still, however, the depreciation figures so derived run far higher than those derived by Galanskii and Phillips, even after the latter are adjusted to include depreciation on "unproductive" capital. The author views these depreciation estimates as one of the weakest points in the current study.

Preservation of Natural Resources

The treatment of natural resources depletion is particularly difficult both conceptually and empirically. There is sentiment for retaining the classical view that natural resources are free and derive such productivity as they embody, at least in the value sense, from the labor and capital necessary to discover and extract them. On the other hand, in the face of growing ecological concern, this view is subject to interpretation or misinterpretation as involving singular negligence toward a crucial social problem. The Office of Business Economics practice of including depletion requirements in profits rather than capital consumption may be construed as reinforcing the classicists' view, although the understandable admixture of concept and convenience involved precludes definiteness in this interpretation.[36]

For present purposes, the depletion allowances afforded to business firms are not appropriate. These allowances are totally legal constructs, devoid of basis upon any social consumption concept. Nor are these allowances retrieved for purposes of adjustment. Rather, public expenditures for the conservation and development of natural and agricultural resources are deemed as the appropriate proximate magnitudes of social consumption. For ease of presentation, data on these public expenditures are presented with general social overhead, rather than with capital consumption.

4 Estimation of Personal Essential Consumption

BLS City Workers' Family Budget

The Bureau of Labor Statistics City Workers' Family Budget embodying the "modest but adequate" standard of living is the budget concept to be used in estimating personal essential consumption.[1] This budget was priced by the BLS several times in the 1946-1970 interval. The average cost of the "goods and services" or the "family consumption" expenditures portion of the budget is given in Table 4-1. The average costs for 1946-1959 are computed directly by taking the mean of the BLS data. Those for 1966-1970 use the average provided by the BLS under the description "urban United States." However, the figures as given by the BLS for total family consumption have been adjusted to delete the increased budget costs due to allowance for homeownership. These increased costs include items such as property taxes, interest, and insurance,[2] which are not essential. Also, this procedure retains a consistency with earlier budgets, which will prove necessary when the personal consumption figure is adjusted for surplus elements in market prices. The method for deleting the homeowner costs for 1966 and 1967 is to subtract the shelter costs for renter families from the shelter costs for all families, and then to subtract this difference from the family consumption total.[3] For 1968 and 1970, rough figures were obtained by applying the ratio of the change in total housing cost in 1967 to total housing cost in 1967 to the 1968 and 1970 total housing cost figures.

The adjusted average cost column includes additions and deductions from the BLS figures. For 1946-1959, the BLS included a category "gifts and contributions" in its goods and services budget. This category amounted to 2.7 percent of the total cost of goods and services in 1946-1951[4] and 2.4 percent in 1959.[5] This category includes all gifts to members outside the family and all contributions to religious or charity organizations. Although a case can be made for inclusion of customary personal gift-giving in essential consumption, there is no case for including church activities and only a weak case for charity activities. Therefore, since no evidence is available concerning the proportion of personal gift-giving in the total, the entire category is excluded from the adjusted average cost. Such an adjustment is unnecessary for 1966 and after, since the category is separated from family consumption in the BLS data.

The BLS in all cases treats the occupational expenses item as a separate figure. These expenses are judged essential and are included in the essential consumption figure. For 1946-1951, the occupational expense addition is $22;[6] for 1959, it is $28;[7] and for 1966-1970, it is $80.[8]

Table 4-1

City Worker's Family Budget, Selected Dates, 1946-1970 (in current dollars)[a]

Date	Average Cost for Specified Location Goods & Services	Description of Location	Adjusted Average Cost
March 1946	$2,517	34 large cities	$2,536
June 1947	2,970	34 large cities	2,912
October 1949	3,244	34 large cities	3,178
October 1950	3,388	34 large cities	3,319
October 1951	3,713	34 large cities	3,635
Autumn 1959	5,165	20 large cities & suburbs	5,069
Family Consumption			
Autumn 1966	$6,851	39 metropolitan & non-metropolitan areas	$6,789
Spring 1967	6,747	39 metropolitan & non-metropolitan areas	6,827
Autumn 1968	7,138	39 metropolitan & non-metropolitan areas	7,218
Spring 1970	7,673	39 metropolitan & non-metropolitan areas	7,753

[a]Source: U.S. Department of Labor, Bureau of Labor Statistics, WORKERS' BUDGETS IN THE U.S.: CITY FAMILIES AND SINGLE PERSONS, 1946 AND 1947, Bulletin 927 (Washington, D.C.: Government Printing Office, 1948), pp. 28-30, and HANDBOOK OF LABOR STATISTICS, 1950 EDITION, Bulletin 1016 (Washington, D.C.: Government Printing Office, 1950), p. 122. Eunice M. Knapp, "City Workers' Family Budget for October 1951," MONTHLY LABOR REVIEW, LXVI (May 1952), 521. Helen H. Lamale and Margaret S. Stotz, "The Interim City Workers' Family Budget," ibid., LXXXIII (August 1960), 787 and 803. Phyllis Groom, "A New City Workers' Family Budget," ibid., XC (November 1967), 3. Jean C. Brackett, "New BLS Budgets Provide Yardsticks for Measuring Family Living Costs," ibid., XCII (April 1969), 8 and 12. Elizabeth Ruiz, "Spring 1970 Cost Estimates of Urban Family Budgets," ibid., XCIV (January 1971), 60.

In two years adjustments were made to align the figures with later BLS methodological procedures and corrections. For 1946, $65 has been added to reflect such a methodological change,[9] and for 1966, a deduction of $142 is necessary for the same reason.[10]

In all cases, the BLS presents separate figures providing for life insurance premiums, income and capitation taxes, and employee social security, disability, and unemployment assessments. These have been omitted here. The services provided by these fees that are judged necessary will be included in the social overhead element of essential social consumption. It would thus be double-counting to include them at this juncture. Finally, sales taxes and other turnover charges and a variety of surplus elements imbedded in market prices remain in the figures to this point and are deleted in Chapter 5.

WPA Maintenance Budget

Prior to 1946, when the Bureau of Labor Statistics first priced the CWFB, there is no readily available budget series commensurate with the CWFB in both the modest but adequate provision and the spatial and temporal scope of the BLS studies. The Heller Committee budgets are rather near the BLS budget conception, but they are limited geographically to San Francisco. The WPA maintenance budget shares the scope of the CWFB through time and space, especially since the BLS cooperated in pricing the budget in 1935 and 1937 and priced it alone for several years thereafter.

The maintenance concept of the WPA budget is clearly more stringent in its provisions than the CWFB. In 1943, the last year that the WPA budget was priced, its 33-city average was $1,593, whereas only three years later the first CWFB pricing averaged $2,536 for thirty-four cities. A relatively small percentage of this change is attributable to price changes insofar as the BLS Consumer Price Index is an appropriate guide. Nor can the change in any part be attributed to secularly increasing social judgment as to what is necessary. Both budgets are based in large part on consumer expenditure studies prior to 1941, and a change in scientific judgment concerning food adequacy was incorporated into the maintenance budget by the BLS as early as 1941.[11]

These same factors, which make it clear that a conceptual change is involved in the 1943-1946 cost differential, contain a saving feature. That is, they allow a rough adjustment to be made upon the WPA budget so that the modest but adequate standard can be approximated for the dates that the maintenance budget was priced. This follows from the implication that the cost differential of the 1943 and 1946 budgets is due to price changes and conceptual upgrading. Therefore, the differential remaining after adjustment for price changes is due to the conceptual revision. Both budgets were priced in March of the respective years. The Consumer Price Index for March 1943 was 122.9, and for March 1946 130.4.[12] Hence, by forming a ratio of 122.9 to 130.4 and multiplying this ratio by the March 1946 budget cost of $2,536, the approximate figure for the CWFB in 1943 is found to be $2,389. By forming a ratio of the $2,389 figure to the 1943 maintenance budget cost of $1,593, an adjustment factor of 1.4997 is determined. This factor rounded to 1.5 is then multiplied by the maintenance budget cost for other years to approximate the CWFB for those years.[13] The average cost of the maintenance budget for available dates and the adjusted average cost for these dates is presented in Table 4-2. For convenience, the personal essential consumption figures at the modest but adequate standard are brought together in Table 4-3. It is worth reiterating that these figures contain surplus elements such as taxes, property incomes, and business wastes that are deleted in Chapter 5.

Table 4-2
WPA Maintenance Budget, Selected Dates, 1935-1943 (in current dollars)[a]

Date	Average Cost	Location Description	Adjusted to CWFB
March 1935	$1,197	59 cities	$1,796
March 1937	1,275	31 cities	1,913
December 1938	1,253	31 large cities	1,880
June and December 1939	1,277	33 large cities	1,916
March 1941	1,302	33 large cities	1,953
June and December 1942	1,535	33 large cities	2,303
March 1943	1,593	33 large cities	2,390

[a]Source: U.S. Works Progress Administration, Division of Social Research, INTERCITY DIFFERENCES IN COSTS OF LIVING IN MARCH 1935, 59 CITIES, Research Monograph 12 (Washington, D.C.: Government Printing Office, 1937), pp. xix and 10. Faith M. Williams, "Living Costs in 1938," MONTHLY LABOR REVIEW, XLVIII (March 1939), 535. "Estimated Intercity Differences in Cost of Living, June 15, 1939," ibid., L (November 1939), 1166. "Estimated Intercity Differences in Cost of Living, December 15, 1939," ibid., LI (April 1940), 572. "Estimated Intercity Differences in Cost of Living, June 15, 1942," ibid., LV (September 1942), 572. "Intercity Differences in Cost of Living, December, 1942," ibid., LVI (April 1943), 746. "Estimated Intercity Differences in Cost of Living, March 15, 1943," ibid., LVII (October 1943), 804-805. Also, U.S. Department of Labor, Bureau of Labor Statistics, HANDBOOK OF LABOR STATISTICS, 1941 EDITION, Bulletin 694 (Washington, D.C.: Government Printing Office, 1941), p. 99.

In all cases, $46.40 has been deducted for life insurance premiums, $15.40 for contributions, and 0.2 percent of the total budget for income and capitation taxes—see U.S. Works Progress Administration, Division of Social Research, INTERCITY DIFFERENCES IN COSTS OF LIVING IN MARCH, 1935, 59 CITIES, pp. 6, 86, and 160.

Table 4-3
Adjusted City Worker's Family Budget for A Four-Person Family, Selected Years, 1935-1970 (in current dollars)[a]

Year	Average Cost	Year	Average Cost
1935	$1,796	1949	$3,178
1937	1,913	1950	3,319
1938	1,880	1951	3,635
1939	1,916	1959	5,069
1941	1,953	1966	6,789
1942	2,303	1967	6,827
1943	2,390	1968	7,218
1946	2,536	1970	7,753
1947	2,912		

[a]Source: Tables 4-1, 4-2, and text.

Adjustments for Family Characteristics

Equivalences for Families of Different Sizes

The CWFB and the WPA maintenance budget represent a specified family consisting of four: husband; wife;. son age thirteen, and daughter age eight. In addition, for the CWFB, the husband and wife are specified to be age thirty-eight and thirty-six, respectively. Hence, some adjustment must be made for families of other sizes. In the earlier literature on consumer budgets, this adjustment was usually viewed in terms of "expenditure units" or "adult male equivalences."[14] For example, the Bureau of Labor Statistics used the following food consumption equivalences in its studies around 1920:[15]

Male	
15 years or over	1.00 equivalent adult male
Female	
15 years or over	.90
Children,	
11 to 14, inclusive	.90
Children,	
7 to 10, inclusive	.75
Children,	
4 to 6, inclusive	.40
Children	
under 4	.15

However, more recent practice has skipped this intermediate stage concentrating on food requirements and developed equivalences for families of different sizes for all expenditures. These total budget equivalences are based on consumer expenditure surveys. The BLS derived an adjustment scale for the original CWFB. By this scale, a family of two persons requires 66 percent of the four-person CWFB; a family of three, 84 percent; a family of five, 114 percent; and a family of six, 128 percent.[16] This scale is based on the consumer expenditure surveys that were used to determine the CWFB through 1951. Kolko estimates the percentage of the CWFB needed by a family of seven or more to be 140 percent. As he points out, however, this percentage is on the conservative side, since the average family size of the group is eight members.[17] For one-person families, the figure of 46 percent derived by the BLS by one of its methods, although not corroborated by the alternative method, may be taken as approximately correct.[18]

A revised scale was later published based on the BLS consumer expenditure survey of 1950. By this scale a two-person husband and wife family, both aged thirty-five to fifty-five, requires 66 percent of the basic CWFB; a three-person family, husband and wife aged thirty-five to fifty-five, child aged six to sixteen, requires 87 percent of the CWFB; and a five-person family, husband and wife aged thirty-five to fifty-five, oldest child aged six to sixteen, requires 120 percent of the CWFB.[19]

Thus, the scale published by the BLS applicable to the CWFB from 1966 distinguishes between the budget needs of families with different characteristics. In particular, sex of head, age of head, and age of children are used to define different family types.[20] Undoubtedly, these distinctions are important for specific purposes such as assaying the needs of the elderly or of low-income families.[21] However, for the gross type of estimation involved in the present study, these differences due to sex and age appear insignificant and safely ignorable. Only the adjustment for family size need be used.

The more recent method based upon consumer expenditure surveys for total expenditures rather than the adult male equivalency practice is adopted here. For each period, 1929-1951, 1952-1959, and 1960-1970, the equivalence scale reflecting BLS current practice is used.

For 1952-1959, since percentages are not available for six- or seven-person families, these must be estimated. In the pre-1952 scale, the increase from a four- to a five-person family and from a five- to six-person family is the same (14 percent). This relation is arbitrarily assumed to prevail for the later scale as well, and the increase of 20 percent from a four- to a five-person family is used as the difference between a five- and a six-person family. Likewise, the ratio of the change from five to six persons and the change from six to seven or more persons in the earlier scale (.85) is used to estimate the percentage for seven or more persons in the later scale. Hence, the percentages for six and for seven or more persons are 140 percent and 157 percent respectively. For one-person families, 48 percent (72 percent of the two-person budget) is used following what Mollie Orshansky alludes to as "recent BLS practice."[22]

For 1960-1970, of the various figures given by the BLS, those adopted are for the family having a husband age thirty-five to fifty-four, wife, and oldest child age six to fifteen.[23] These family types correspond most closely to the ones used in the earlier equivalence scales. For convenience, the percentages to be used for all three periods are drawn together in Table 4-4.

Table 4-4
Portion of the Four-Person CWFB Necessary for Families of Other Sizes, Three Time Period Divisions, 1929-1970 (in percent)[a]

Family Size	1929-1951	1952-1959	1960-1970
One	46%	48%	38%
Two	66	66	61
Three	84	87	83
Five	114	120	115
Six	128	140	130[b]
Seven or More	140	157	

[a]For derivation procedure and references, see text.
[b]For six or more persons.

Farm and Nonfarm Residency

In deriving budget standards it is common practice to adjust the nonfarm cost of the budget for those residing on farms. A large part of this adjustment rests on income in kind on the farm in the form of homegrown food and housing provisions.[24] The remaining portion of the adjustment reflects different living requirements, consumption standards, and price differentials.[25] For the use made of the budget concept in this study, no adjustment for the income in kind phenomenon is necessary. The level of purchasing power in terms of money income of the farm subgroup is not of interest here. Rather, the search is for a measure of essential consumption in aggregate terms to relate to the level of gross production. And, the Office of Business Economics' production statistics includes estimates of farm income in kind. Further, the portion reflecting differential living standards is of dubious value. For one thing, there is a danger in comparing budget costs of different living standards that dates at least to Irving Fisher's "ideal index number."[26] And, it is apparent from Koffsky's discussion that much of this standard of living differential rests upon a lower level of living on the farm.[27] The only substantive reason for adjustment appears to be price differentials beyond those reflecting differential consumption standards. No adjustment is attempted for this factor here. Judging from the relative size of the farm population and existing price differentials, this apparently places only a very minor qualification on the present analysis.

Personal Essential Consumption in
Current Market Prices

Estimates can now be derived for personal essential consumption at market prices for the selected years in the 1929-1970 period. Tables 4-5 through 4-9 contain the data used in the estimation procedure. Table 4-5 shows the number of households containing various numbers of persons for various years in the period. The Bureau of the Census' household category is used rather than its family category. A household is defined as a number of persons who live and eat together as a unit.[28] This functional point of view is more appropriate for present purposes than one stressing familial or legalistic relationships.

Also shown in Table 4-5 is the population in units which the Bureau of the Census regards as "quais-households" or, in later usage, "group quarters." These are units in which there is no identified household head, being for the most part institutions such as prisons and sanitariums. Neither the number of these quasi-households nor their population are included in the household category.

Table 4-6 contains estimates of the number of households by size for the years in which personal esssential consumption budgets are available. These estimates are taken directly from Table 4-5 or, where necessary, computed from Table 4-5 by straight-line interpolation. The number of quasi-households is estimated through 1959 by dividing the population in such units by seven, and

Table 4-5
Population Residency Characteristics, Selected Years, 1940-1968 (in millions)[a]

| | Households by Number of Persons per Household | | | | | | | |
Date	1	2	3	4	5	6	7 or more	Number of Quasi-Households
April 1940	2.7	8.6	7.8	6.3	4.0	2.4	3.0	0.5
April 1949	3.4	11.5	10.2	8.1	4.4	2.3	2.2	0.5
March 1950	3.9	12.4	10.0	7.9	4.6	2.3	2.3	0.4
March 1960	6.9	14.6	9.9	9.3	6.1	3.0	2.9	0.4
March 1966	9.0	16.6	9.9	9.4	6.2	3.4	3.4	0.4
March 1967	9.1	16.7	10.3	9.5	6.2	3.5	3.5	0.5
March 1968	9.7	17.3	10.5	9.6	6.3	3.6	3.5	0.5

[a]Source: U.S. Department of Commerce, Bureau of the Census, CURRENT POPULATION REPORTS, Series P-20, no. 26 and no. 33, POPULATION CHARACTERISTICS (Washington, D.C.: Government Printing Office, 1950 and 1951), pp. 12 and 14 and 12 and 14, respectively. Also, U.S. Department of Commerce, Bureau of the Census, CURRENT POPULATION REPORTS, Series P-20, no. 106, no. 164, no. 173, and no. 191, HOUSEHOLD AND FAMILY CHARACTERISTICS (Washington, D.C.: Government Printing Office, 1961, 1967, 1968, and 1969), pp. 13, 11, 14, and 78, respectively.

Table 4-6
Number of Households by Size, Selected Years, 1935-1970 (in millions)[a]

Year	1	2	3	4	5	6	7 or or more[b]
1935	2.3	7.0	6.5	5.3	3.8	2.5	4.0
1937	2.5	7.7	7.0	5.7	3.9	2.4	3.8
1938	2.5	8.0	7.3	5.9	3.9	2.4	3.7
1939	2.6	8.3	7.5	6.1	4.0	2.4	3.6
1941	2.8	8.9	8.1	6.5	4.0	2.4	3.4
1942	2.9	9.2	8.3	6.7	4.1	2.4	3.4
1943	2.9	9.6	8.6	6.9	4.1	2.4	3.2
1946	3.2	10.5	9.4	7.5	4.2	2.3	3.0
1947	3.3	10.8	9.7	7.7	4.3	2.3	2.9
1949	3.4	11.5	10.2	8.1	4.4	2.3	2.7
1950	3.9	12.4	10.0	7.9	4.6	2.3	2.7
1951	4.2	12.6	10.0	8.0	4.8	2.4	2.8
1959	6.8	14.4	9.9	9.2	6.0	2.9	3.2
1966	9.0	16.6	9.9	9.4	6.2	7.2[c]	NA
1967	9.1	16.7	10.3	9.5	6.2	7.5[c]	NA
1968	9.7	17.3	10.5	9.6	6.3	7.6[c]	NA
1970	10.5	18.0	11.1	9.8	6.4	7.9[c]	NA

[a]Taken directly or via interpolation from Table 4-5.

[b]Includes "quasi-households."

[c]Six or more person households, including "quasi-households."

for 1966-1970 by dividing by six. These numbers are then included under the descriptive headings seven or more persons and six or more persons, respectively.

Table 4-7 contains the CWFB cost for families of various sizes in the relevant years. These estimates are computed directly from the CWFB cost for a four-person family (Table 4-3), and the percentages of this budget required for families of other sizes (Table 4-4).

Table 4-8 shows the estimated aggregate essential consumption at market prices for the selected years. These figures are computed by multiplying the number of households of a given size (Table 4-6) by the necessary budget cost for that given size (Table 4-7). Summing these figures for households of various sizes yields estimates of aggregate personal essential consumption at market prices ranging from $53.1 billion in 1935 to $400.1 billion in 1970. In Table 4-9, personal essential consumption is estimated for the remaining years in the 1929-1970 period by interpolation and price change ratios from Table 4-8.

Table 4-7
Cost of Adjusted CWFB for Family Units of Various Sizes, Selected Years, 1935-1970 (in current prices)[a]

	Budget Cost by Persons in Family						
Year	1	2	3	4	5	6	7 or more
1935	$ 826	$1,185	$1,509	$1,796	$2,047	$ 2,299	$2,514
1937	880	1,263	1,607	1,913	2,181	2,449	2,678
1938	865	1,241	1,579	1,880	2,143	2,406	2,632
1939	881	1,265	1,609	1,916	2,184	2,452	2,682
1941	898	1,289	1,641	1,953	2,226	2,500	2,734
1942	1,059	1,520	1,935	2,303	2,625	2,948	3,224
1943	1,099	1,577	2,008	2,390	2,725	3,059	3,346
1946	1,167	1,674	2,130	2,536	2,891	3,246	3,550
1947	1,340	1,922	2,446	2,912	3,320	3,727	4,077
1949	1,462	2,097	2,670	3,178	3,623	4,068	4,449
1950	1,527	2,191	2,788	3,319	3,784	4,248	4,647
1951	1,672	2,399	3,053	3,635	4,144	4,653	5,089
1959	2,433	3,346	4,410	5,069	6,083	7.097	7,958
1966	2,580	4,141	5,635	6,789	7,807	8,826[b]	NA
1967	2,594	4,164	5,666	6,827	7,851	8,875[b]	NA
1968	2,743	4,403	5,991	7,218	8,301	9,383[b]	NA
1970	2,946	4,729	6,435	7,753	8,916	10,079[b]	NA

[a]Derived from Tables 4-3 and 4-4.

[b]For six or more persons.

Table 4-8
Aggregate Personal Essential Consumption in Current Market Prices, Selected Years, 1935-1970 (in billions)[a]

Year				Aggregate Essential Consumption for Each Household Size				
	1	2	3	4	5	6	7 or more	Total
1935	$ 1.90	$ 8.30	$ 9.81	$ 9.52	$ 7.78	$ 5.75	$10.06	$,53.1
1937	2.20	9.73	11.25	10.90	8.51	5.88	10.18	58.7
1938	2.16	9.93	11.53	11.09	8.36	5.77	9.74	58.6
1939	2.29	10.50	12.07	11.69	8.74	5.88	9.66	60.8
1941	2.51	11.47	13.29	12.69	8.90	6.00	9.30	64.2
1942	3.07	13.98	16.06	15.43	10.76	7.08	10.96	77.3
1943	3.19	15.14	17.27	16.49	11.17	7.34	10.71	81.3
1946	3.73	17.58	20.02	19.02	12.14	7.47	10.65	90.6
1947	4.42	20.76	23.73	22.42	14.28	8.57	11.82	106.0
1949	4.97	24.12	27.23	25.74	15.94	9.36	12.01	119.4
1950	5.96	27.17	27.88	26.22	17.41	9.77	12.55	127.1
1951	7.02	30.23	30.53	29.08	19.89	11.17	14.25	142.2
1959	16.54	48.18	43.66	46.63	36.50	20.58	25.47	237.6
1966	23.22	68.74	55.79	63.82	48.40	63.55[b]	NA	323.5
1967	23.61	69.54	58.36	64.95	48.68	66.56[b]	NA	331.7
1968	26.61	76.17	62.91	69.29	52.30	71.31[b]	NA	358.6
1970	30.93	85.12	71.43	75.98	57.06	79.62[b]	NA	400.1

[a]Derived from Tables 4-6 and 4-7.

[b]For six or more person households.

Table 4-9

Aggregate Personal Essential Consumption in Current Market Prices, Annually, 1929-1970 (in billions)[a]

Year	PEC	Year	PEC	Year	PEC
1929	$66.5	1943	$ 81.3	1957	$213.6
1930	64.8	1944	83.2	1958	225.5
1931	59.0	1945	85.0	1959	237.6
1932	53.0	1946	90.6	1960	249.9
1933	50.2	1947	106.0	1961	262.2
1934	52.0	1948	115.6	1962	274.5
1935	53.1	1949	119.4	1963	286.8
1936	53.8	1950	127.1	1964	299.1
1937	58.7	1951	142.2	1965	311.4
1938	58.6	1952	154.1	1966	323.5
1939	60.8	1953	166.0	1967	331.7
1940	61.5	1954	177.9	1968	358.6
1941	64.2	1955	189.8	1969	379.4
1942	77.3	1956	201.7	1970	400.1

[a]This table is derived from Table 4-6 by using either ratios of price changes or straight line interpolation. The latter method tends to create less distortion during periods of stably trending prices and significant population growth. It is used for the period after 1951. The price changes method is used prior to 1951 due to the up and down price movements and the lack of any blank space on the order of that of 1952-1958. The Consumer Price Index used is that of the U.S. Department of Labor, Bureau of Labor Statistics, CHANGES IN COST OF LIVING IN LARGE CITIES IN THE UNITED STATES, 1913-41, Bulletin 699 (Washington, D.C.: Government Printing Office, 1941), p. 43, and HANDBOOK OF LABOR STATISTICS, 1950 EDITION, Bulletin 1016 (Washington, D.C.: Government Printing Office, 1950), p. 100.

5

Estimation of Social
Essential Consumption

Essential Social Overhead Consumption
Pure Social Overhead Consumption

As explained in Chapter 3 above, several items of government expenditure are for all practical purposes exhausted in the year of provision. That is, they are necessary to maintain or support the extant productive capacity but do not increase this capacity.

Included in this category are the provision of general government administration, conduct of international affairs, maintenance of civilian safety, sanitation, and postal systems, and support of resource preservation[1] and recreation facilities. The relevant figures for 1952-1970 are shown in Table 5-1. These are taken directly from a number of *Survey of Current Business* issues. Purchases of goods and services figures are used thus omitting transfer payments and overlapping expenditures due to intergovernmental transfers. Surpluses of government enterprises have been subtracted and subsidies added when they occur in a relevant category.

The omission of personal transfers and the inclusion of subsidies warrants a word of explanation. Personal consumption is already included by using budget cost and population estimates. Therefore, it would be double-counting to include transfer payments that are to provide income for personal consumption. However, the subsidies presumably have the effect of keeping consumer prices lower. Therefore, the subsidies do not appear in the personal consumption estimates.

Prior to 1952 this convenient breakdown is not available for government expenditures. Therefore, estimates must be made for these years. The method for doing so here is first to compute the average ratio of pure social overhead consumption to nondefense government purchases of goods and services for the 1952-1970 period. Then, this ratio is applied to nondefense purchases for the 1929-1951 period to estimate pure social consumption.

From Table 5-2, the ratio of pure social overhead expenditures to total nondefense purchases is found to average 26.6 percent for the 1952-1970 period. This percentage is applied to nondefense purchases in Table 5-3 to arrive at estimates for pure social consumption for the 1929-1951 period.

For years prior to 1939, the Department of Commerce does not divide government purchases as to defense or nondefense. However, Francis M. Bator estimates defense purchases to have been $0.7 billion in 1929.[2] This figure is

Table 5-1

Pure Social Overhead Consumption, Annually, 1952-1970 (in billions of current dollars)[a]

Year	General Government and International Affairs		Civilian Safety, Sanitation, and Postal Services		Resource Preservation and Recreation		Total
	Federal	State/Local	Federal	State/Local	Federal	State/Local	
1952	$1.64	$ 1.57	$0.86	$ 2.77	$1.51	$0.92	$ 9.3
1953	1.43	1.66	0.64	2.84	1.31	0.63	8.5
1954	1.37	1.84	0.41	3.15	1.29	1.05	9.1
1955	1.54	1.98	0.54	3.40	1.03	1.16	9.7
1956	1.58	2.23	0.67	3.74	1.47	1.33	11.0
1957	1.49	2.61	0.63	4.04	2.08	1.50	12.4
1958	1.55	2.91	0.78	4.37	2.38	1.62	13.6
1959	1.62	3.23	0.62	4.69	1.91	1.74	13.8
1960	1.99	3.35	0.73	5.02	2.61	1.98	15.7
1961	2.05	3.57	0.93	5.37	2.34	2.16	16.4
1962	2.27	3.88	0.93	5.66	2.35	2.13	17.2
1963	2.50	4.25	0.73	6.07	2.48	2.45	18.5
1964	2.80	4.89	0.85	6.57	2.40	2.66	20.2
1965	2.93	5.81	0.90	6.97	2.41	2.63	21.7
1966	2.70	5.94	1.11	7.56	2.80	2.86	23.0
1967	2.60	7.02	1.29	8.32	2.91	3.35	25.5
1968	2.69	9.05	0.96	9.49	2.58	3.67	28.4
1969	3.31	10.10	1.27	10.35	2.41	4.11	32.6
1970	3.82	10.70	2.33	12.28	2.84	4.31	36.3

[a]Source: U.S. Department of Commerce, Office of Business Economics, THE NATIONAL INCOME AND PRODUCT ACCOUNTS OF THE UNITED STATES, 1929-1965, STATISTICAL TABLES (Washington, D.C.: Government Printing Office, 1966), pp. 60-69; SURVEY OF CURRENT BUSINESS, L (July 1970), 33, and LI (July 1971), 29-30.

used for 1929 and for interpolation to estimate the defense and nondefense distribution of government purchases for the 1930-1938 period.

Mixed Social Consumption and Social Investment

As explained in Chapter 3, some categories of government expenditures contain both consumption and investment elements. As shown in Table 5-4, there are three such categories to be considered: expenditures for transportation and public utilities, education, and health and hospitals.

Table 5-2

Government Purchases of Goods and Services, All Levels, Annually, 1952-1970 (in billions of current dollars)[a]

Year	Total Purchases	Nondefense Purchases	Pure Social Overhead Purchases	Ratio
1952	$ 74.66	$ 28.73	$ 9.3	0.324
1953	81.65	32.98	8.5	0.258
1954	74.80	33.60	9.1	0.271
1955	74.20	35.64	9.7	0.272
1956	78.58	38.25	11.0	0.288
1957	86.12	41.90	12.4	0.296
1958	94.16	48.26	13.6	0.282
1959	97.01	50.96	13.8	0.271
1960	99.62	54.68	15.7	0.287
1961	107.63	59.80	16.4	0.274
1962	117.12	65.54	17.2	0.262
1963	122.48	71.72	18.5	0.258
1964	128.91	78.92	20.2	0.256
1965	136.23	86.08	21.7	0.252
1966	156.81	96.13	23.0	0.239
1967	180.08	107.74	25.5	0.237
1968	199.56	121.54	28.4	0.234
1969	209.71	131.30	32.6	0.248
1970	219.39	144.04	36.3	0.252

[a]Source: Table 5-1 and U.S. Department of Commerce, Office of Business Economics, THE NATIONAL INCOME AND PRODUCT ACCOUNTS OF THE UNITED STATES, 1929-1965, STATISTICAL TABLES (Washington, D.C: Government Printing Office, 1966), pp. 2-3; SURVEY OF CURRENT BUSINESS, L (July 1970), 17, and LI (July 1971), 13.

For these three categories, rough arbiters are devised to assign expenditures to either consumption or investment. In all three instances, a lack of information and, more importantly, the existence of lags between the year of expenditure and the year of production prevent the assignment from proceeding on a year-to-year basis. Hence, the period is arbitrarily divided into two subperiods, 1929-1950 and 1950-1970. Ratios using the first and last year of each subperiod are used for each year therein.

Transportation and Public Utilities

There exists no reliable basis for assigning transportation to consumption or investment on a physical quantity basis. The data available on road mileage are sketchy and unreliable, especially prior to 1939.[3] Moreover, no reliable data are available on municipal road mileage prior to around 1950, and it is not possible

Table 5-3
Pure Social Overhead Consumption, Annually, 1929-1951 (in billions of current dollars)[a]

Year	Total Purchases	Nondefense Purchases	Pure Social Consumption Purchases
1929	$ 8.50	$ 7.80	$2.1
1930	9.20	8.44	2.2
1931	9.22	8.41	2.2
1932	8.09	7.22	1.9
1933	8.05	7.13	1.9
1934	9.78	8.80	2.3
1935	10.01	8.98	2.4
1936	11.97	10.88	2.9
1937	11.86	10.72	2.9
1938	12.98	11.78	3.1
1939	13.33	12.08	3.2
1940	14.00	11.79	3.1
1941	24.77	11.02	2.9
1942	59.59	10.23	2.7
1943	88.56	8.82	2.3
1944	96.54	9.11	2.4
1945	82.28	8.77	2.3
1946	27.01	12.27	3.3
1947	25.11	16.04	4.3
1948	31.55	20.82	5.5
1949	37.85	24.58	6.5
1950	37.90	23.81	6.3
1951	59.13	25.54	6.8

[a]Source: U.S. Department of Commerce, Office of Business Economics, THE NATIONAL INCOME AND PRODUCT ACCOUNTS OF THE UNITED STATES, 1929-1965, STATISTICAL TABLES (Washington, D.C.: Government Printing Office, 1966), pp. 2-3. For 1929-1938, nondefense purchases are interpolated using Bator's estimate of defense spending for 1929. Francis M. Bator, THE QUESTION OF GOVERNMENT SPENDING: PUBLIC NEEDS AND PRIVATE WANTS (New York: Harper and Brothers, 1960), p. 138.

to infer such mileage from highway extension and access roads which enter municipal limits.[4] Data on the growth of air transport volumes are similarly scarce prior to 1946.[5]

The method of assignment used involves changes in constant dollar GNP. The rationale for this procedure is that of technical proportionality. Given some increase in physical production, it may be supposed that a roughly proportionate increase occurs in the facilities for transporting this produce. Also, since several means of transport are involved, there is some room for technical change and

Table 5-4

Government Purchases of Goods and Services, Mixed Consumption and Investment Items, All Levels, Annually, 1952-1970 (in billions of current dollars)[a]

Year	Transportation and Utilities	Education[b]	Health and Hospitals[b]
1952	$ 5.21	$ 8.35	$ 3.30
1953	5.53	9.37	3.36
1954	6.25	10.64	3.34
1955	6.84	11.93	3.53
1956	7.45	13.04	3.86
1957	8.41	14.17	4.32
1958	9.46	15.97	4.69
1959	9.91	17.24	5.09
1960	9.96	18.71	5.42
1961	10.90	20.67	5.83
1962	11.02	22.12	6.27
1963	11.80	24.15	6.66
1964	12.62	26.69	7.27
1965	13.69	29.06	7.81
1966	14.63	35.18	8.67
1967	16.04	39.54	9.95
1968	17.39	43.83	11.05
1969	17.68	48.53	12.08
1970	19.05	54.14	12.77

[a]Source: U.S. Department of Commerce, Office of Business Economics, THE NATIONAL INCOME AND PRODUCT ACCOUNTS OF THE UNITED STATES, 1929-1965, STATISTICAL TABLES (Washington, D.C.: Government Printing Office, 1966), pp. 60-69; SURVEY OF CURRENT BUSINESS, L (July 1970), 33, and LI (July 1971), 29-30.

[b]Includes purchases of goods and services incurred in the provision of educational, health, and hospital services through the Veterans Administration.

varying proportions in this assumption, for example, the shift from rail to air transport.

Since reliable data do not exist for physical volumes of public utilities output, they are included with transportation and the proportionality assumption applied to them as well. The fact that the assumption is somewhat more dubious in this instance is mitigated by the small volume of expenditures net of revenue for public utilities.

Transportation and public utility expenditures are given in column one of Table 5-4. Transportation includes highway, air, and water transport expenditures; public utilities include expenditures for transit, electricity, water, and gas services. In all cases, only purchases of goods and services and subsidies are used. Transfer payments are excluded. Moreover, surpluses of government enterprises in the relevant categories, especially electric utilities, are subtracted from the purchases figure.

GNP in 1958 dollars equaled $203.6 billion in 1929, $355.3 billion in 1950, and $720.0 billion in 1970. Hence, 57.3 percent of expenditures in the 1929-1950 subperiod are assigned to consumption and 49.3 percent in the 1950-1970 subperiod. The volumes assigned to social consumption in this fashion for 1952-1970 are shown in column one of Table 5-5.

Education

The second category of mixed consumption and investment is found in the area of expenditures for education. These expenditures are assigned to consumption or investment via changes in the educational attainment of labor force partici-

Table 5-5

Social Essential Consumption for Mixed Categories, Annually, 1952-1970 (in billions of current dollars)[a]

Year	Transportation and Utilities	Education	Health and Hospitals	Total
1952	$2.57	$ 4.83	$1.83	$ 9.23
1953	2.73	5.42	1.86	10.01
1954	3.08	6.15	1.85	11.08
1955	3.37	6.90	1.96	12.23
1956	3.67	7.54	2.14	13.35
1957	4.15	8.19	2.40	14.74
1958	4.66	9.23	2.60	16.49
1959	4.89	9.96	2.82	17.67
1960	4.91	10.81	3.01	18.73
1961	5.37	11.95	3.24	20.56
1962	5.43	12.79	3.48	21.70
1963	5.82	13.96	3.70	23.48
1964	6.22	15.43	4.03	25.68
1965	6.75	16.80	4.33	27.88
1966	7.21	20.33	4.81	32.35
1967	7.91	22.85	5.52	36.28
1968	8.57	25.33	6.13	40.03
1969	8.72	28.05	6.70	43.47
1970	9.39	31.29	7.09	47.77

[a]For derivation procedure, see text.

pants. The reasoning involved is that the size and educational levels of the labor force at the beginning of a period are part of the productive plant and must be maintained. This maintenance is, of course, a part of essential consumption. However, any increase in the size or level of educational attainment of the labor force is to be considered investment. The labor force is used rather than the population as a whole because educational expenditures on those persons not entering the labor force are properly considered a part of the surplus.

Total governmental purchases of goods and services related to education are given in column two of Table 5-4. Expenditures for educational services provided via the Veterans Administration are included. Transfer payments are omitted since the budget for personal consumption includes educational expenses.

The civilian labor force was 49.2 million in 1929, 62.2 million in 1950, and 82.7 million in 1970.[6] The median school years completed for the population as a whole was 8.6 in 1940,[7] 9.3 in 1950, and 12.1 in 1970. By multiplying the median completion figure by the labor force size for each year, an index representing educational attainment of the labor force is formed. The ratios of this index for 1929-1950 (.731) and for 1950-1970 (.578) are then used as the consumption portion for each year in each subperiod. Column two of Table 5-5 shows essential social consumption for education for the 1952-1970 period.

Health and Hospitals

The final category involving elements of both consumption and investment is that of health and hospital services. As with education, there is no mandate for assignment in this category according to changes in real GNP. That is, there is not sufficient reason to assume proportionality between health services and real output. Therefore, assignment in this category is made on the basis of changes in hospital admissions. Total hospital admissions were approximately 7.16 million in 1931,[8] 16.75 million in 1950, and 30.19 million in 1969.[9] Assignment ratios on this basis are 0.427 for 1929-1950 and 0.555 for 1950-1970. Column three of Table 5-5 gives essential social consumption for health and hospital services for 1952-1970.

1929-1951

As noted above in regard to pure social consumption, the convenient breakdown on government expenditures is not available prior to 1952. Estimates of expenditures in the 1929-1951 period for the three mixed consumption and investment categories are derived by the same method as in the pure consumption case. The percentage share of nondefense purchases of goods and services for the three categories is assumed to be the same for 1929-1951 as for 1952-1970. From Table 5-6, the average percentage share in the 1952-1970 period for transportation and public utilities is computed to be 17.1 percent, for education 33.9 percent, and for health and hospitals 9.7 percent. These percentages are translated into dollar estimates for these items in the 1929-1951 period in Table 5-7. The assignment percentages derived above are applied to these magnitudes in Table 5-7 to arrive at social consumption estimates. In all cases, the year 1950 is included in the 1950-1970 period.

Essential Capital Consumption

As discussed in Chapter 3 above, the estimates of essential capital consumption are based upon the work of Allan H. Young.[10] The procedure is to first form ratios of Young's straight line, historical cost, F service lives depreciation series for nonfinancial corporations to the Office of Business Economics' depreciation series for these corporations. Then, these ratios are applied to the Office of Business Economics' series for total capital consumption to arrive at estimates of essential capital consumption. These operations are summarized in Tables 5-8 and 5-9.

Total Essential Consumption and the
Adjustment for Surplus Elements
Imbedded in Market Prices

In Table 5-10, personal essential consumption and social essential consumption are combined to form total essential consumption in current market prices. There remains in these estimates of total essential consumption a variety of surplus elements. These are imbedded in the structure of market prices in such a way as to prohibit their direct exclusion in the manner of excluding payroll taxes, life insurance premiums, and governmental transfer payments. The method for dealing with these imbedded surplus elements is first to form a ratio of their sum to GNP for a given year. Then, this proportion is deleted from the total essential consumption estimate for that year. These operations are summarized in Tables 5-11 through 5-15. In Table 5-15, the final estimate of total essential consumption is given and converted to 1958 prices.

Table 5-6
Government Purchases of Goods and Services, Selected Categories, All Levels, Annually, 1952-1970 (in billions of current dollars and as percent of nondefense purchases)[a]

Year	Nondefense Purchases	Transportation and Utilities		Education		Health and Hospitals	
1952	$ 28.73	$ 5.21	18.1%	$ 8.35	29.1%	$ 3.30	11.5%
1953	32.98	5.53	16.8	9.37	28.4	3.36	10.2
1954	33.60	6.25	18.6	10.64	31.2	3.34	9.9
1955	35.64	6.84	19.2	11.93	33.5	3.53	9.9
1956	38.25	7.45	19.5	13.04	34.1	3.86	10.1
1957	41.90	8.41	20.1	14.17	33.8	4.32	10.3
1958	48.26	9.46	19.6	15.97	33.1	4.69	9.7
1959	50.96	9.91	19.4	17.24	33.8	5.09	10.0
1960	54.68	9.96	18.2	18.71	34.2	5.42	9.9
1961	59.80	10.90	18.2	20.67	34.6	5.83	9.7
1962	65.54	11.02	16.8	22.12	33.8	6.27	9.6
1963	71.72	11.80	16.5	24.15	33.7	6.66	9.3
1964	78.92	12.62	16.0	26.69	33.8	7.27	9.2
1965	86.08	13.69	15.9	29.06	33.8	7.81	9.1
1966	96.13	14.63	15.2	35.18	36.6	8.67	9.0
1967	107.74	16.04	14.9	39.54	36.7	9.95	9.2
1968	121.54	17.39	14.3	43.83	36.1	11.05	9.1
1969	131.30	17.68	13.5	48.53	37.0	12.08	9.2
1970	144.04	19.05	13.2	54.14	37.6	12.77	8.9

[a]Source: Tables 5-2 and 5-4.

Table 5-7

Estimates of Government Purchases for Mixed Categories and Amounts Assigned to Essential Consumption, Annually, 1929-1951 (in billions of current dollars)[a]

Year	Transportation and Utilities		Education		Health & Hospitals		Total Assigned to Social Consumption
	Estimate	Social Consumption	Estimate	Social Consumption	Estimate	Social Consumption	
1929	$1.33	$0.76	$2.64	$1.93	$0.76	$0.32	$3.01
1930	1.44	0.83	2.86	2.09	0.82	0.35	3.27
1931	1.44	0.83	2.85	2.08	0.82	0.35	3.26
1932	1.23	0.70	2.45	1.79	0.70	0.30	2.79
1933	1.22	0.70	2.42	1.77	0.69	0.29	2.76
1934	1.50	0.86	2.98	2.18	0.85	0.36	3.40
1935	1.54	0.88	3.04	2.22	0.87	0.37	3.47
1936	1.86	1.07	3.69	2.70	1.06	0.45	4.22
1937	1.83	1.02	3.63	2.65	1.04	0.44	4.11
1938	2.01	1.15	3.99	2.92	1.14	0.49	4.56
1939	2.07	1.19	4.10	3.00	1.17	0.50	4.69
1940	2.02	1.16	4.00	2.92	1.14	0.49	4.57
1941	1.88	1.08	3.74	2.73	1.07	0.46	4.27
1942	1.75	1.00	3.47	2.54	0.99	0.42	3.96
1943	1.51	0.87	2.99	2.19	0.86	0.37	3.43
1944	1.56	0.89	3.09	2.26	0.88	0.38	3.53
1945	1.50	0.86	2.97	2.17	0.85	0.36	3.39

1946	2.10	1.20	4.16	3.04	1.19	0.51	4.75
1947	2.74	1.57	5.44	3.98	1.56	0.67	6.22
1948	3.56	2.04	7.06	5.16	2.02	0.86	8.06
1949	4.20	2.41	8.33	6.09	2.38	1.02	9.52
1950	4.07	2.01	8.07	4.66	2.31	1.28	7.95
1951	4.37	2.15	8.66	5.01	2.48	1.38	8.54

[a]For derivation procedure, see text.

Table 5-8
Alternative Depreciation Measures, Nonfinancial Corporations, Annually, 1929-1970 (in billions of current dollars)[a]

Year	Straight Line[b] Depreciation	Office of Business Economics Depreciation	Ratio
1929	$ 4.4	$ 4.1	1.07
1930	4.6	4.2	1.10
1931	4.5	4.2	1.07
1932	4.5	3.9	1.15
1933	4.3	3.7	1.16
1934	4.2	3.6	1.17
1935	4.1	3.5	1.17
1936	4.1	3.5	1.17
1937	4.3	3.6	1.19
1938	4.4	3.7	1.22
1939	4.4	3.7	1.19
1940	4.4	3.7	1.19
1941	4.5	4.1	1.12
1942	4.7	5.0	0.94
1943	4.6	5.3	0.87
1944	4.5	6.0	0.75
1945	4.6	6.3	0.73
1946	4.9	4.6	1.07
1947	5.5	5.7	0.96
1948	6.4	6.8	0.94
1949	7.4	7.8	0.95
1950	8.5	8.6	0.99
1951	9.5	10.0	0.95
1952	10.5	11.2	0.94
1953	11.4	12.8	0.89
1954	12.1	14.5	0.83
1955	13.1	16.8	0.78
1956	14.3	18.3	0.78
1957	15.6	20.2	0.77
1958	16.7	21.2	0.79
1959	17.7	22.6	0.78
1960	19.1	24.0	0.80
1961	20.4	25.1	0.81
1962	21.8	28.8	0.76
1963	23.4	30.4	0.77
1964	25.1	32.2	0.78
1965	27.2	34.5	0.79

Table 5-8 (cont.)

Year	Straight Line[b] Depreciation	Office of Business Economics Depreciation	Ratio
1966	29.9	37.0	0.81
1967	32.9	40.7	0.81
1968	35.5	44.2	0.80
1969	38.7	48.3	0.80
1970	42.1	52.8	0.80

[a]This table is based upon the methods and data of Allan H. Young, "Alternative Estimates of Corporate Depreciation and Profits: Parts I and II," SURVEY OF CURRENT BUSINESS, XLVIII (April 1968), 17-28, and (May 1968), 16-28. Additional data used are from the update of Young's calculations, "Alternative Estimates of Corporate Depreciation and Profits, 1965-70," ibid., LII (January 1972), 34-35.

[b]This is one of several depreciation measures used by Young. It is based upon "historical [original] cost" and the service lives of the 1942 Bulletin F of the Internal Revenue Service.

Table 5-9

Essential Capital Consumption, Annually, 1929-1970 (in billions of current dollars)

Year	Office of Busines Economics Capital Consumption[a]	Essential Capital Consumption[b]
1929	$ 7.9	$ 8.5
1930	8.0	8.8
1931	7.9	8.5
1932	7.4	8.5
1933	7.0	8.1
1934	6.8	8.0
1935	6.9	8.1
1936	7.0	8.2
1937	7.2	8.6
1938	7.3	8.9
1939	7.3	8.7
1940	7.5	8.9
1941	8.2	9.2
1942	9.8	9.2
1943	10.3	9.0
1944	11.0	8.3
1945	11.3	8.2
1946	9.9	10.6
1947	12.2	11.7
1948	14.5	13.6
1949	16.6	15.8

Table 5-9 (cont.)

Year	Office of Business Economics Capital Consumption[a]	Essential Capital Consumption[b]
1950	18.3	18.1
1951	21.2	20.1
1952	23.2	21.8
1953	25.7	22.9
1954	28.2	23.4
1955	31.5	24.6
1956	34.1	26.6
1957	37.1	28.6
1958	38.9	30.7
1959	41.4	32.3
1960	43.4	34.7
1961	45.2	36.6
1962	50.0	38.0
1963	52.6	40.5
1964	56.0	43.7
1965	59.6	47.1
1966	63.9	51.8
1967	68.9	55.8
1968	74.5	59.6
1969	81.1	64.9
1970	87.6	70.1

[a]Source: U.S. Department of Commerce, Office of Business Economics, THE NATIONAL INCOME AND PRODUCT ACCOUNTS OF THE UNITED STATES, 1929-1965, STATISTICAL TABLES (Washington, D.C.: Government Printing Office, 1966), pp. 12-13; and SURVEY OF CURRENT BUSINESS, L (July 1970), 19, and LI (July 1971), 15.

[b]Computed by applying the ratios from Table 5-8 to the Office of Business Economics capital consumption series.

Table 5-10
Total Essential Consumption in Current Market Prices, Annually, 1929-1970 (in billions)[a]

Year	Personal	Pure Social	Mixed Social	Capital	Total
1929	$ 66.5	$ 2.1	$ 3.0	$ 8.5	$ 80.1
1930	64.8	2.2	3.3	8.8	79.1
1931	59.0	2.2	3.3	8.5	73.0
1932	53.0	1.9	2.8	8.5	66.2
1933	50.2	1.9	2.8	8.5	63.0
1934	52.0	2.3	3.4	8.0	65.7

Table 5-10 (cont.)

Year	Personal	Pure Social	Mixed Social	Capital	Total
1935	53.1	2.4	3.5	8.1	67.1
1936	53.8	2.9	4.2	8.2	69.1
1937	58.7	2.9	4.1	8.6	74.3
1938	58.6	3.1	4.6	8.9	78.1
1939	60.8	3.2	4.7	8.7	77.4
1940	61.5	3.1	4.6	8.9	78.1
1941	64.2	2.9	4.3	9.2	80.6
1942	77.3	2.7	4.0	9.2	93.2
1943	81.3	2.3	3.4	9.0	96.0
1944	83.2	2.4	3.5	8.3	97.4
1945	85.0	2.3	3.4	8.2	98.9
1946	90.6	3.3	4.8	10.6	109.3
1947	106.0	4.3	6.2	11.7	128.2
1948	115.6	5.5	8.1	13.6	142.8
1949	119.4	6.5	9.5	15.8	151.2
1950	127.1	6.3	8.0	18.1	159.5
1951	142.2	6.8	8.5	20.1	177.6
1952	154.1	9.3	9.2	21.8	194.4
1953	166.0	8.5	10.0	22.9	207.4
1954	177.9	9.1	11.1	23.4	221.5
1955	189.8	9.7	12.2	24.6	236.3
1956	201.7	11.0	13.4	26.6	252.7
1957	213.6	12.4	14.7	28.6	269.3
1958	225.5	13.6	16.5	30.7	286.3
1959	237.6	13.8	17.7	32.3	301.4
1960	249.9	15.7	18.7	34.7	319.0
1961	262.2	16.4	20.6	36.6	335.8
1962	274.5	17.2	21.7	38.0	351.4
1963	286.8	18.5	23.5	40.5	369.3
1964	299.1	20.2	25.7	43.7	388.7
1965	311.4	21.7	27.9	47.1	408.1
1966	323.5	23.0	32.4	51.8	430.7
1967	331.7	25.5	36.3	55.8	449.3
1968	358.6	28.4	40.0	59.6	486.6
1969	379.4	32.6	43.5	64.9	520.4
1970	400.1	36.3	47.8	70.1	554.3

[a]Source: Tables 4-9, 5-1, 5-3, 5-5, 5-7, and 5-9.

Table 5-11

Miscellaneous Government Revenue, All Levels, Annually, 1929-1970 (in billions of current dollars)[a]

Year	Indirect Business Taxes & Non-Taxes	Non-Payroll Personal Taxes & Non-Taxes	Employer Social Insurance Contributions	Year	Indirect Business Taxes & Non-Taxes	Non-Payroll Personal Taxes & Non-Taxes	Employer Social Insurance Contributions
1929	$ 7.0	$1.3	$0.1	1950	$23.4	$ 2.5	$ 4.0
1930	7.1	1.4	0.1	1951	25.2	2.8	4.8
1931	6.9	1.3	0.1	1952	27.2	3.0	4.9
1932	6.7	1.2	0.1	1953	29.6	3.3	4.9
1933	7.0	1.0	0.1	1954	29.4	3.6	5.2
1934	7.8	1.1	0.1	1955	32.1	3.8	5.9
1935	8.2	1.2	0.2	1956	34.9	4.4	6.8
1936	8.7	1.4	0.4	1957	37.3	4.9	7.8
1937	9.2	1.4	1.2	1958	38.5	5.1	8.0
1938	9.1	1.4	1.4	1959	41.4	5.7	9.7
1939	9.3	1.4	1.5	1960	45.2	6.4	11.4
1940	10.0	1.4	1.6	1961	47.7	7.1	11.8
1941	11.3	1.4	2.0	1962	51.5	7.7	13.7
1942	11.7	1.6	2.3	1963	54.7	8.3	15.0
1943	12.7	1.6	2.7	1964	58.5	9.5	15.4
1944	14.2	1.7	2.9	1965	62.6	10.3	16.0
1945	15.5	2.0	3.8	1966	65.6	11.3	20.3
1946	17.1	1.9	4.0	1967	70.4	12.4	21.9
1947	18.4	2.2	3.6	1968	78.6	13.4	24.4
1948	20.1	2.4	3.0	1969	85.6	15.0	27.8
1949	21.3	2.5	3.5	1970	92.9	16.3	29.6

[a]Source: U.S. Department of Commerce, Office of Business Economics, THE NATIONAL INCOME AND PRODUCT ACCOUNTS OF THE UNITED STATES, 1929-1970, STATISTICAL TABLES (Washington, D.C.: Government Printing Office, 1966), pp. 14-15, 52-53, and 54-55, and SURVEY OF CURRENT BUSINESS, L (July 1970), 20, 29, and 30, and L1 (July 1971), 16, 25, and 26.

Table 5-12

Wages and Salaries in Surplus Industries, Annually, 1929-1970 (in billions of current dollars)[a]

Year	Finance, Insurance Real Estate	Advertising[b]	Year	Finance, Insurance, Real Estate	Advertising[b]
1929	$2.9	$0.9	1950	$ 5.8	$ 3.7
1930	2.7	0.8	1951	6.4	4.2
1931	2.5	1.0	1952	6.9	4.7
1932	2.1	1.0	1953	7.5	5.0
1933	1.9	1.0	1954	8.1	5.3
1934	2.0	1.1	1955	8.9	6.0
1935	2.1	1.1	1956	9.6	6.4
1936	2.2	1.1	1957	10.3	6.7
1937	2.4	1.2	1958	10.9	6.7
1938	2.3	1.2	1959	11.8	7.3
1939	2.4	1.3	1960	12.4	7.8
1940	2.5	1.4	1961	13.3	7.7
1941	2.6	1.5	1962	13.9	8.0
1942	2.7	1.4	1963	14.7	8.5
1943	2.8	1.6	1964	15.8	9.2
1944	3.0	1.8	1965	16.8	9.9
1945	3.3	1.9	1966	18.0	10.8
1946	4.1	2.2	1967	19.8	11.0
1947	4.5	2.8	1968	22.3	11.8
1948	5.1	3.2	1969	24.9	12.7
1949	5.3	3.4	1970	27.0	12.8

[a]Source: U.S. Department of Commerce, Office of Business Economics, THE NATIONAL INCOME AND PRODUCT ACCOUNTS OF THE UNITED STATES, 1929-1970, STATISTICAL TABLES (Washington, D.C.: Government Printing Office, 1966), pp. 94-97, and SURVEY OF CURRENT BUSINESS, L (July 1970), 39, and LI (July 1971), 35.

[b]These figures are based on the approximate ratio (65 percent) of wages and salaries to national income in the service industries. The ratio is applied to the advertising expenditures given in U.S. Department of Commerce, Bureau of the Census, STATISTICAL ABSTRACT OF THE UNITED STATES, 1971 EDITION (Washington, D.C.: Government Printing Office, 1971), p. 745. Some years were filled in via interpolation.

Table 5-13
Surplus Elements Imbedded in Market Prices, Annually, 1929-1970 (in billions of current dollars)[a]

Year	Misc. Gov't Revenue	Profits[b]	Net Business Interest	Personal Rental Income	Surplus Wages & Salaries
1929	$ 8.4	$ 22.1	$ 4.7	$ 5.4	$ 3.8
1930	8.6	17.9	4.9	4.8	3.6
1931	8.3	12.2	5.0	3.8	3.5
1932	8.0	7.5	4.6	2.7	3.1
1933	8.1	7.3	4.1	2.0	2.9
1934	9.0	10.5	4.1	1.7	3.1
1935	9.6	12.9	4.1	1.7	3.2
1936	10.5	15.4	3.8	1.8	3.3
1937	11.8	17.2	3.7	2.1	3.6
1938	11.9	15.0	3.6	2.6	3.5
1939	12.2	16.6	3.5	2.7	3.7
1940	13.0	20.6	3.3	2.9	3.9
1941	14.7	27.9	3.2	3.5	4.1
1942	15.6	36.1	3.1	4.5	4.1
1943	17.0	41.8	2.7	5.1	4.4
1944	18.8	42.3	2.3	5.4	4.8
1945	21.3	38.3	2.2	5.6	5.2
1946	23.0	38.3	1.5	6.6	6.3
1947	24.2	46.7	1.9	7.1	7.3
1948	25.5	57.6	1.8	8.0	8.3
1949	27.3	56.2	1.9	8.4	8.7
1950	29.9	65.4	2.0	9.4	9.5
1951	32.8	74.4	2.3	10.3	10.6
1952	35.5	73.6	2.6	11.5	11.6
1953	37.8	75.4	2.8	12.7	12.5
1954	38.2	76.2	3.6	13.6	13.4
1955	41.8	88.7	4.1	13.9	14.9
1956	46.1	90.9	4.6	14.3	16.0
1957	50.0	93.7	5.6	14.8	17.0
1958	51.6	91.8	6.8	15.4	17.6
1959	56.8	104.8	7.1	15.6	19.1
1960	63.0	104.9	8.4	15.8	20.2
1961	66.6	107.2	10.0	16.0	21.0
1962	72.9	118.1	11.6	16.7	21.9
1963	78.0	124.3	13.8	17.1	23.2
1964	83.4	135.6	15.5	17.7	25.0

Table 5-13 (cont.)

Year	Misc. Gov't Revenue	Profits[b]	Net Business Interest	Personal Rental Income	Surplus Wages & Salaries
1965	88.9	147.8	17.8	18.3	26.7
1966	97.2	161.7	21.4	20.0	28.8
1967	102.7	163.1	24.4	21.1	30.8
1968	116.4	174.9	26.9	21.2	34.1
1969	128.4	176.6	30.0	22.6	37.6
1970	138.8	175.1	33.0	23.3	39.8

[a]Tables 5-11 and 5-12; U.S. Department of Commerce, Office of Business Economics, THE NATIONAL INCOME AND PRODUCT ACCOUNTS OF THE UNITED STATES, 1929-1970, STATISTICAL TABLES (Washington, D.C.: Government Printing Office, 1966), pp. 12-13 and 14-15; SURVEY OF CURRENT BUSINESS, L (July 1970), 19 and 20, and LI (July 1971), 15 and 16.

[b]This includes corporate profits, capital consumption, and 25 percent of the income of unincorporated enterprises. See Edward C. Budd, "Treatment of Distributive Shares," in A CRITIQUE OF THE UNITED STATES INCOME AND PRODUCT ACCOUNTS, STUDIES IN INCOME AND WEALTH, Vol. XXII, National Bureau of Economic Research (Princeton, New Jersey: Princeton University Press, 1958), pp. 356-357; and Edward F. Denison, "Income Types and the Size Distribution," AMERICAN ECONOMIC REVIEW/SUPPLEMENT, XLIV (May 1954), 256.

Table 5-14
Ratio of Surplus Elements Imbedded in Market Prices to GNP, Annually, 1929-1970 (in billions)[a]

Year	GNP	Surplus Elements	Ratio	Year	GNP	Surplus Elements	Ratio
1929	$103.1	$ 44.4	0.431	1950	$284.8	$116.6	0.408
1930	90.4	39.8	0.440	1951	328.4	130.4	0.397
1931	75.8	32.8	0.433	1952	345.5	134.8	0.390
1932	58.0	25.9	0.447	1953	364.6	141.2	0.387
1933	55.6	24.4	0.439	1954	364.8	145.0	0.397
1934	65.1	28.4	0.436	1955	398.0	163.4	0.411
1935	72.2	31.5	0.436	1956	419.2	171.9	0.410
1936	82.5	34.8	0.422	1957	441.1	181.1	0.411
1937	90.4	38.4	0.425	1958	447.3	183.2	0.410
1938	84.7	36.6	0.432	1959	483.7	203.4	0.421
1939	90.5	38.7	0.428	1960	503.7	212.3	0.421
1940	100.0	43.7	0.437	1961	520.1	220.8	0.424
1941	124.5	53.4	0.429	1962	560.3	241.2	0.430
1942	157.9	63.4	0.402	1963	590.5	256.4	0.434
1943	191.6	71.0	0.371	1964	631.7	277.2	0.439
1944	210.1	73.6	0.350	1965	681.2	299.5	0.440
1945	211.9	72.6	0.343	1966	749.9	329.1	0.439
1946	208.5	75.7	0.363	1967	793.9	342.1	0.431
1947	231.3	87.2	0.377	1968	864.2	373.5	0.432
1948	257.6	101.2	0.393	1969	929.1	395.2	0.425
1949	256.5	102.5	0.400	1970	974.1	410.0	0.421

[a]Source: Table 5-14; U.S. Department of Commerce, Office of Business Economics, THE NATIONAL INCOME AND PRODUCT ACCOUNTS OF THE UNITED STATES, 1929-1970, STATISTICAL TABLES (Washington, D.C.: Government Printing Office, 1966), pp. 2-3; and SURVEY OF CURRENT BUSINESS, L (July 1970), 17, and LI (July 1971), 13.

Table 5-15
Total Essential Consumption, Annually, 1929-1970 (in billions of current and 1958 dollars)[a]

Year	$ Current	$ 1958	Year	$ Current	$ 1958
1929	45.6	90.1	1950	94.4	117.7
1930	44.3	89.9	1951	107.1	125.1
1931	41.4	92.4	1952	118.5	135.4
1932	36.6	91.0	1953	127.1	143.9
1933	35.3	89.8	1954	133.6	149.1
1934	37.1	87.9	1955	139.2	153.1
1935	37.8	88.7	1956	149.1	158.6
1936	39.9	93.7	1957	158.6	162.7
1937	42.7	96.0	1958	168.9	168.9
1938	42.7	97.3	1959	174.5	171.8
1939	44.3	102.5	1960	184.7	178.8
1940	44.0	100.2	1961	193.4	184.9
1941	46.0	97.5	1962	200.3	189.3
1942	55.7	105.1	1963	209.0	195.0
1943	60.4	106.3	1964	218.1	200.3
1944	63.3	108.8	1965	228.5	206.0
1945	65.0	108.9	1966	241.6	212.1
1946	69.6	104.3	1967	255.7	217.4
1947	79.9	107.1	1968	276.4	226.0
1948	86.7	108.9	1969	299.2	233.4
1949	90.7	114.7	1970	320.9	237.2

[a]Source: Tables 5-10 and 5-14; U.S. Department of Commerce, Office of Business Economics, THE NATIONAL INCOME AND PRODUCT ACCOUNTS OF THE UNITED STATES, 1929-1970, Statistical Tables (Washington, D.C.: Government Printing Office, 1966), pp. 158-159; and SURVEY OF CURRENT BUSINESS, L (July 1970), 47, and LI (July 1971), 43.

6

Excess Capacity, Unemployment, and Potential Output

The next task of the current study is the estimation of potential output. Potential output may be viewed as the maximum feasible output attainable from the given social productive plant. The usual method of estimating potential output is to estimate the percentage utilization of productive capacity and then to adjust the actual output figure accordingly.

Discussions of potential and full employment output and the gap or shortfall of actual output therefrom vary widely in character. However, two central, usually exclusive, elements common to all such discussions are underutilization of the capital stock and unemployment of the labor force. These two elements are usually viewed solely in quantitative terms; that is, the quantity utilized is compared to the quantity available. Such treatment ignores the more qualitative elements involved, such as the underutilization of scale economies, wasteful product differentiation, planned obsolescence, and malutilization of scientific and technological knowledge. These latter elements have long been recognized in the underworld literature, but have not been systematically incorporated into mainstream economics nor had their impact subjected to quantitative measurement.[1] Indeed, it seems that the discipline has taken to heart the words of its paramount modern figure:

... I see no reason to suppose that the existing system seriously misemploys the factors of production which are in use. ... It is in determining the volume, not the direction, of actual employment that the existing system has broken down.[2]

Thus, with no empirical leg to stand on in this qualitative area, the current study is restricted to the traditional quantitatively oriented approach.

Excess capacity is usually used in reference to the physical capital stock. To move from estimates of excess capacity to potential output, it is necessary to ascertain that unemployed labor exists that could man the unused capital. The present chapter reviews the concepts and estimates of excess capacity and unemployment and some of the potential output estimates derived directly or indirectly therefrom. This review is brief and selective. The following chapter deals with the basis adopted for estimating potential output and the estimates thus derived.

Excess Capacity

On the Definition of Capacity

Capacity, and therefore excess capacity, is difficult to define meaningfully. This ambiguity stems from the juxtaposition and interrelation of the social and technical factors involved. To illustrate, consider the three basic definitional points of view cited by Loeb from which capacity may be approached:

The capacity of the existing plant with operation governed by existing customs and traditions.
The capacity of the existing plant if production were limited solely by physical factors and knowledge (i.e., resources, manpower, and technology).
The capacity of the nation to produce goods and services if full advantage were taken of existing resources, manpower, and knowledge.[3]

The latter two are both technical in nature. They differ from each other in that the former is limited to the extant productive plant while the latter "substitutes for [the extant plant] a non-existent, yet possible plant." This possible plant would include the replacement of obsolete capital at an optimum technical rate and the use of modern management methods. The first definition differs from the latter two in that social elements, such as the customary number of shifts and seasonal demand fluctuations, are used as an additional limiting factor upon capacity.

The third definition is the more dynamic of the three, drawing scientific and technical advance into the definition of capacity. In Loeb's view, the "study of capacity from such a point of view would be a running inventory of our approach to perfection."[4] It is probably the concept Veblen has in mind when, possibly somewhat tongue in cheek, he estimates:

... that under ordinary [peacetime] conditions of businesslike management, the habitual net production is fairly to be rated at something like one-fourth of the industrial community's productive capacity; presumably under that figure rather than over.[5]

It is not clear from his argument whether or not Veblen's net product excludes spurious output such as selling costs. At any rate, he does not undertake a systematic empirical study of the matter. In fact, he takes a dubious view of the possibility of such an undertaking given the "existing circumstances of ownership and control." And, whether or not Veblen had in mind a definition of this third type, no one purports to have made a quantitative study on such a basis.

In the study directed by Loeb, the second definition whereby capacity is limited by existing plant and technical feasibility was used. The objective of the study was:

... to ascertain America's capacity to produce goods and services regardless of customary or institutional practices, which can be changed at will. [That is, to] indicate what the American people might expect to have for consumption, given the existing equipment, if production were directed toward the satisfaction of the needs and wants of the population and limited only by our resources, manpower, and knowledge.[6]

The authors recognize that the second definition sometimes distorts this objective, as when a technical bottleneck in the production process exists for which a remedy is readily available. Also, they note that some elements of custom enter in, notably in determining the hours of work for labor.[7]

The authors of the well-known Brookings Institution study used the first definition. Their definition of capacity is output "attainable under the *practical operating conditions* which exist." In the aggregate, this allows for "sustained simultaneous operation" that precludes supernumerary shifts and overtime. Their estimate is based upon customary workday hours, workweek days, and daily shifts. The estimate of capacity is lowered to the extent of usual seasonal fluctuations of output and shutdowns for maintenance and repair. No attempt is made to incorporate ideal conditions nor to allow for the degree of utilization of scale economies, technology, or other such qualitative factors. In fact, they explicitly limit themselves to underproduction caused by insufficient aggregate demand:

We are not attempting to calculate productive performances that might be brought about under ideal conditions but simply to measure how much more product we could turn out if the demand of the market were such as to keep our plant and labor employed as fully as they could be under accepted hours of labor and with proper standards of plant maintenance.[8]

More comments are made on the Loeb and Brookings studies below in relation to potential output. Enough has been said to this point to illustrate the differences involved in the three definitions of capacity. It is not at all clear which basis is most suitable for present purposes. Stated extremely, the technical definitions strip the capacity concept of its social content and render it of dubious value to the analysis of production, which is after all a social process. Stated likewise, the custom oriented definition casts an aura of inscrutability around tradition, myth, and customary practice. This veil of their being the natural order of things robs the capacity concept of utility in the analysis of social change. This is particularly true in relation to the provision of a benchmark for comparison with actual practice and the formulation of normative prescriptions for social change. Apparently, the acceptable ground must lie somewhere in between these extremes, but just where the current author would be hard pressed to specify.

Fortunately, the choice is not for the author to make. All available studies, except the one directed by Loeb, implicitly or explicitly accept the customary basis of the Brookings study. For example, Donald Streever defines capacity as:

> The physical volume of goods and services that can be produced during a given period when productive facilities are utilized to their maximum under normal operating conditions. . . . The concept is intended to be practical and the normal workweek is therefore implicit. . . . The length of the workweek varies from industry to industry. . . . Some industries are continuous process industries; others operate only one shift. What is important in the present context [is] the role of the normal workweek as a practical limit on production. . . . The concept of capacity [herein] is in agreement with the Brookings concept.[9]

Other writers interject the custom element more surreptitiously. Daniel Creamer purports to avoid the problems of customary versus technical factors in his definition of capacity by using capital-output ratios:

> The approach here proposed is the analysis of the relationship of capital to output. Such an analysis would avoid the technical problems inherent in the measurement of physical capacity. . . . The procedure suggested is to establish . . . a fixed capital-output ratio for a benchmark year which independent evidence indicates was a period when capacity was virtually fully utilized.[10]

Obviously, "independent evidence" cannot indicate full utilization of capacity if capacity remains undefined. Creamer's benchmark year and independent evidence is one of the peak periods of the postwar business cycle (1948). Essentially then, customary practices of the year 1948 are incorporated into Creamer's analysis.

Finally, the McGraw-Hill method of viewing capacity as being in the eyes of the respondent undoubtedly incorporates the custom element. The McGraw-Hill surveys simply ask the respondent business executive to state his plant's percentage change in capacity as "measured in physical volume" during a given period and the percentage of its total capacity used at a point in time. No definitions of capacity are provided.[11] Thus, the respondent is left to define workweek and similar factors upon which capacity rests. One may justifiably suppose that past practice in such matters would weigh heavily in the respondent's deliberation.

Estimates of Excess Capacity

Capacity utilization estimates are generally limited to manufacturing, sometimes including mining, since therein lies the bulk of capital stock. The extensive Brookings study estimates capacity utilization ratios for manufacturing averaging 80 percent for 1925-1929 and 83 percent for 1929 alone. For mining, the estimate is 83.4 percent both for the 1925-1929 average and the peak year 1929.[12] As noted above, the Brookings study was based upon practically attainable and customary capacity rather than technically rated capacity. Also, completely idle plants were judged obsolete and omitted from the capacity estimate.

Donald Streever's study for manufacturing and mining covers the period 1920-1955. He takes the Brookings' 83 percent utilization rate as his benchmark. By assuming equal degrees of utilization in 1923 and 1948, he computes a "scaling factor" which is then applied to annual changes in the capital stock to arrive at the change in capacity. By adding the change in capacity to the benchmark figure, he arrives at an estimate of total capacity.[13]

Baran and Sweezy use Streever's capacity index and the Federal Reserve Board's index of industrial production[14] to compute a capacity utilization index for the 1920s and 1930s. For 1920-1929, this index ranges from a 1920 and 1923 high of 94 percent to a 1921 low of 65 percent. The average for 1920-1929 is 84.5 percent and for 1925-1929 85.6 percent. For 1930-1939, the index ranges from a 1932 low of 42 percent to 83 percent in 1937. The average for the 1930-1939 period is 63.4 percent.[15] Extending Baran and Sweezy's method through the 1940-1955 period yields a range from 136 percent in 1943 to 78 percent in 1949 and 1954. The average for 1940-1955 is 97.4 percent, for 1940-1949 104.3 percent, and for 1950-1955 85.8 percent. The percentages in excess of 100 percent indicate emergency, forced draft operating rates which exceed the normal full capacity rates.

It is interesting to note that such forced draft production did not occur during the Korean War. The capacity utilization index based on Streever's figures is 89 percent, 90 percent, 87 percent, and 88 percent for the four-year period 1950-1953. As Lewis H. Robb points out, this is in part due to the permanent warfare state established during the Cold War in which Pentagon policy has been to maintain permanent reserve capacity for military preparations.

Robb's capacity utilization index for 1952 is 55 percent. He assumes 100 percent utilization in 1943 despite noting idle capacity in that year due to the nonproportionality caused by the military buildup. He reasons that capacity increased by 60 percent in the 1943-1952 period based on the U.S. Department of Commerce estimate that a 50 percent increase occurred in the 1945-1952 period.

Robb discounts the forced draft argument often used to explain the failure of the Federal Reserve Board's production index to reach its 1943 level by 1952. He reasons that the 1943 higher average weekly work hours and the entry into the labor force of those not normally employed is more than offset by the ten million in the armed services in 1943, the natural increase of the labor force by one million annually, and the productive increases of the postwar period.[16]

Other capacity utilization indices are not directly comparable with those given above since they assume full utilization for some year in the early 1950s.

Using the capital-output ratio method and assuming 100 percent utilization in 1948 and 1953, Daniel Creamer estimates a 1957 utilization rate for manufacturing of 89 percent.[17] In a later publication and using the same method for all manufacturing except newspapers, Creamer estimates utilization rates of 97 percent in 1955, 91 percent in 1956, 88 percent in 1957, 87 percent in 1958, 94 percent in 1959, 93 percent in 1960, and 92 percent in 1961.[18] Creamer's estimates in all cases are for peak operation periods during the year.

A variety of authors derive a utilization index by using the ratio of the Federal Reserve Board's index of manufacturing production to the McGraw-Hill index of capacity. These indices vary somewhat according to the particular publication issue of the two agencies used. Later publication revisions and differences between calendar time operating rates account for these differences. Thus, Robert P. Ulin estimates capacity utilization rates of 100 percent for 1950, 94 percent for 1952, 82 percent for 1953, and 81 percent for 1954.[19] William F. Butler's figures yield rates of 100 percent for 1950, 100 percent for 1951, 97 percent for 1952, 99 percent for 1953, 89 percent for 1954, 93 percent for 1955, 89 percent for 1956, and 85 percent for 1957.[20] Baran and Sweezy estimate rates of 100 percent for 1952, 103 percent for 1951, 99 percent for 1952, 98 percent for 1953, 87 percent for 1954, 92 percent for 1955, 89 percent for 1956, 85 percent for 1957, 76 percent for 1958, 81 percent for 1959, 81 percent for 1960, 80 percent for 1961, 83 percent for 1962, and 83 percent for 1963.[21]

Finally, Alice Bourneuf computes the averages of the McGraw-Hill and F. de Leeuw capacity utilization indices. The McGraw-Hill index averaged 93 percent for 1949-1952, 89 percent for 1953-1955, 79 percent for 1956-1958, 76 percent for 1959-1962, and 84 percent for the entire 1949-1962 period. Professor de Leeuw's index averaged 87 percent for 1949-1952, 89 percent for 1953-1955, 83 percent for 1956-1958, 84 percent for 1959-1962, and 85 percent for 1949-1962.[22]

Although this list could be expanded, it is long enough to indicate the general magnitude of excess capacity. Whether or not one can precisely distinguish equilibrium and disequilibrium excess capacity,[23] it is apparent that something on the order of 10 to 15 percent of capacity, conservatively defined, remains idle in peacetime conditions. Moreover, the entirety of this idle capacity is surely no accident. McGraw-Hill's respondents at year end 1954 were operating at an average rate of 84 percent of capacity and would have *preferred* an average rate of 89 percent.[24] Similarly, in September, 1958, they would have preferred a rate of 90 percent to their actual rate of 82 percent of capacity.[25]

Unemployment

The other side of the coin concerning the gap between actual and potential output is the labor supply. Essentially, the question is whether or not unemployed manpower exists to operate the idle capital capacity. It is not necessary to undertake an extensive review of available manpower *vis-à-vis* excess capacity, since this was done in the Brookings study and corroborated by the study directed by Loeb and the later findings of Robb.

Moreover, such an extensive search is unnecessary to deny any claim that labor shortages cause the excess capacity. This can be done by noting that the percentage of the labor force unemployed moves in phase with the percentage of excess capacity, not contrary to it. The average unemployment rate of the civilian labor force as of November 1 of each year was 4.5 percent for 1953-1955, 5.3 percent for 1956-1958, and 5.9 percent for 1952-1962.[26] Recalling from above that the excess capacity percentages for these years showed similar upward movement indicates that a labor shortage was not the cause for such movement.

Moreover, the official unemployment percentage understates the actual rate of those willing but unable to find work. Strand and Dernburg compute gap unemployment rates based on the estimated size of the labor force participating under high (3 percent) and low (4 percent) full employment conditions. The high full employment gap averaged 6.1 percent for 1953-1955, 6.8 percent for 1956-1958, and 9.2 percent for 1959-1962. The low full employment gap averaged 5.2 percent, 5.9 percent, and 8.3 percent respectively for the same periods.[27]

Finally, that many of these unemployed may be structurally unemployed and lack the necessary skills for operating the unutilized capital is a true but self-defeating argument. The textbooks, even the advanced ones, indicate that were the system functioning effectively, such disproportionality between requisite and available skills would be corrected. To explain excess capacity by denying that such correction is forthcoming is to admit that the disproportionality of the anarchist system of capitalist production inherently underutilizes its productive potential.

Potential Output

Early Studies

The Brookings Study. Potential output studies seek to estimate the level of production that would be forthcoming in a given period if full utilization, variously defined, of capital and human resources were attained. The pioneering and most comprehensive works in the area are the Brookings Institution and Loeb studies. Both surveyed the degree of utilization of capacity in all economic sectors and compared the underutilization of capital capacity with available labor supply and possible technical bottlenecks to assure proportionality in their potential output estimates. The divergence of the two estimates is largely attributable to the approach used in measuring capacity.[28]

The Brookings study estimates the utilization of practical capacity for all sectors, that is, agriculture, transportation, merchandising, and construction as well as mining and manufacturing, to have been 80 percent in 1929.[29] In seeking to ascertain whether or not labor was the limiting factor that prevented full utilization of capacity, the authors surveyed unemployed or underemployed labor in the various economic sectors. Consistent with their goal of determining "practically attainable" production, the authors did not seek to

... present an idealized picture of the potential labor power which might be put to work if we had an improved scheme of economic organization, better labor management, stronger incentives for workers, or a perfect placement system. ... We are attempting to measure the productive capacity of such labor as was at hand but was used to an amount less than it would have been able and willing to render if a larger demand had been forthcoming from the labor market.[30]

In other words, the authors did not seek to measure the volume of labor that would have been available had full employment or a higher degree of proportionality in production been sustained. Even with this limited measure, however, the authors found sufficient available labor to meet the volume needed for full capacity utilization of the productive plant.[31]

In making their final estimation of potential output, the authors also allowed for aggregate disproportionality, bottlenecks, and obsolete equipment not previously excluded with idle plants. To do so, they defined full capacity as 95 percent of the practically attainable capacity. With these "reasonable allowances for failures of co-ordination," their final estimate is that production in 1929 could have been at a minimum 19 percent greater than it actually was.[32] Applying this figure to actual GNP in 1929 and converting to 1958 dollars yields an estimate of $242.5 billion for potential output in 1929.

The Loeb Study. The study directed by Loeb was similar in most respects to the Brookings study. Excess capacity was surveyed for all sectors and matched with the available labor supply to assure that a labor shortage was not a limiting factor. There were, however, two major differences. First, as discussed above, the authors used a more liberal, but not the most liberal, definition of capacity. Second, the authors used an estimate of actual consumer wants and needs in deriving their estimates of capacity. To do so, they used the results of consumer expenditure surveys to estimate the volume of consumer demand for each sector that would have been forthcoming had the population possessed the requisite purchasing power. These "budget" items were then compared with productive capacity in the various lines of production. In cases where productive capacity exceeded the budget need, the capacity was deemed available for use in other areas.[33]

Since they used a capacity concept based on existing plant and methods of production without allowance for technological change, replacement of obsolete equipment, potential labor force participants not participating, planned obsolescence, or other qualitative factors, the authors considered their budget capacity to be "*a minimum estimate of practical capacity* available for the production of desired goods and services."

Their potential output figures amount to a potential 45 percent increase over actual output for 1929, a 59 percent increase in 1930, 75 percent in 1931, 101 percent in 1932, and 86 percent in 1944.[34] Applying these percentages to constant dollar GNP for the respective years yields potential outputs in 1958 dollars of $295.2 billion for 1929, $291.8 billion for 1930, $296.3 billion for 1931, $289.8 billion for 1932, and $263.2 billion for 1933. The significant figure for comparison is the first, which shows a potential output for 1929 over $50 billion greater than that implied by the Brookings study.

Later Studies

During the hot wars period, 1940-1953, the attention of economists centered on the problems of conversion and reconversion of resource allocation. Soon thereafter, however, the carryover progressive thought that produced the Employment Act of 1946 and the concern eventually evoked by the stagnation in the U.S. in comparison to the expansions in Western Europe, Japan, and the Soviet Union combined to renew interest in the level of economic activity and the rate of economic growth. In this surge of interest, although no inventories matching the scope of the two studies discussed above were conducted, there arose a variety of potential output and full employment estimates and concomitant shortfalls, gaps, and deficits.

Keyserling's Estimates of Maximum Output. One of the earliest and most persistent analysts in this regard is Leon H. Keyserling and his Washington-based organization, the Conference on Economic Progress. Whether or not he deserves the "growthmanship" charge so often leveled at him, there is no doubt that Keyserling has been extraordinarily tenacious and consistent in his advocacy of economic growth. In a series of monographs and articles throughout the 1950s and 1960s, he repeated his central themes of maximum employment and growth, the shortfall therefrom, and the social problems which could be ameliorated with the unused potential. Indeed, as late as 1968 and in the face of growing doubt as to the efficacy of steadily increasing GNP in the area of solving social problems, he remains committed to economic growth as the "problem of problems."[35]

Keyserling's method throughout this period has been first to select a period when actual production roughly equaled potential production, then to compute the rate of growth necessary to maintain full employment by summing the percentage increases in productivity per worker and in the civilian labor force. His full employment criterion allows for frictional unemployment somewhere near 3 percent. His necessary growth rate represents a

... sufficient annual rate of growth in G.N.P. to provide full use of growth in labor force, plant and productivity under conditions of maximum employment and production.[36]

Keyserling cautions early on that this method of estimating potential output yields conservative results. The rate of growth derived in this manner, in his opinion,

... is a conservative estimate of the minimum growth in total output that would have been required to maintain full employment and full production. ... It is not an estimate of our full ability to expand total output through the most effective use of our technology, and through the incentive to productivity generated by a full employment environment.[37]

Using his "conservative" growth rate estimate, Keyserling has at various times estimated the cumulative shortfalls or "national economic deficits" for specified periods. For 1929-1953, he estimates a cumulative shortfall of $914 billion in 1953 prices. This estimate is based upon a 3.5 percent growth rate for potential output applied to the 1929 actual production level. The 3.5 percent rate is composed of a 2.4 percent productivity increase and a 1.1 percent labor force increase.[38]

Using the same method, but incorporating changes in the productivity and labor force annual rates of increase, Keyserling computes a cumulative shortfall for 1953 to midyear 1964 of $549.4 billion in 1963 prices.[39] This estimate was later revised to incorporate the latter half of 1964 and amounted to $590 billion, again in 1963 prices.[40] Later, another revision incorporated 1965 and 1966. He estimates the shortfall for 1953-1966 in 1965 prices to have been $700 billion.[41]

Keyserling utilizes this analysis to project the level of GNP required in some future year to assure full employment. Thus, he estimates that GNP by 1970 would have had to increase by $177 billion in 1965 prices over the actual GNP of 1966.[42] Similarly, he estimates that full employment in 1975 would require a GNP of from $1,105 to $1,140 billion in 1965 prices.[43]

Finally, Keyserling expresses the shortfall or production deficiency for selected years as a percentage of maximum production. For 1953, this estimate was 0.3 percent; for 1955, 2.8 percent; for 1959, 9.4 percent; for 1962, 11.2 percent; and for 1963, 11.9 percent.[44] Applying these percentages to the Office of Business Economics' GNP figures in 1958 prices yields the following maximum output estimates: $414.0 billion in 1953; $450.6 billion in 1955; $525.3 billion in 1959; $596.6 billion in 1962; and $625.4 billion in 1963.

Knowles' Estimate of Potential GNP. Another set of potential output estimates is the one prepared by James W. Knowles for the Joint Economic Committee. Knowles originally covered the period 1909-1960, but later extended his estimates to 1965. His estimates are derived from a macabre econometric model involving potential and actual labor inputs, average annual workhours, capital-labor ratios, average capital vintage, and productivity ratios.

Knowles does not attempt to measure capacity output and acknowledges that his measure of potential output falls short of such output:

... The potential is a measure of the optimum or best practice which it is believed the economy is capable of sustaining on the average, year after year, without running into serious instability of employment, output, or prices. It is, in a word, a measure of what would be reasonably good performance of the economy, maintaining a stable relationship between output and capacity. ... No attempt was made ... to measure the ultimate capacity of the economy. It is clear only that it must be much higher than the measure of potential output arrived at in this study.[45]

An unemployment rate of 4 percent was used by Knowles in computing his estimates. This figure was selected due to its use in past Joint Economic Committee staff studies and historical data that showed unemployment averaging 4 percent "in periods of high prosperity." A cyclical variable incorporating demand fluctuations was also used in the model. This limiting adjustment represents the "so-called mix effect" that demand shifts alter the volume of potential output derivable from fixed stocks of capital and labor due to changes in input proportions and output-input ratios. Finally, the volumes of the potential labor force, capital stock, and age of the capital stock assume their actual historical values. That is, no adjustment is made on these factors to estimate what their volumes would have been had relatively full use of resources been continuously achieved.[46] Knowles' estimates of potential output, converted to 1958 prices, are presented in Table 6-1.

Department of Commerce Estimates of Potential GNP. The Bureau of the Census of the U.S. Department of Commerce provides estimates of potential GNP in its publication, *Business Conditions Digest*. These estimates are derived by applying a trend line through the actual level of GNP in midyear 1955. The growth rates used in this trend line are 3.5 percent from 1955 to the fourth quarter of 1962, 3.75 percent from fourth quarter 1962 to fourth quarter 1965, 4 percent for fourth quarter 1965 to fourth quarter 1969, and 4.3 percent thereafter.[47] These growth rates are based on expected potential labor supply and productivity changes. The full employment criterion of 4 percent to 1969 and 3.8 percent thereafter follows the definition of the Council of Economic Advisers.[48]

Estimates of potential GNP derived from the Department of Commerce figures are given in Table 6-2. The Department of Commerce gives its estimates

Table 6-1
Knowles' Estimates of Potential GNP, Selected Years, 1929-1965 (in billions of 1958 dollars)[a]

Year	Potential GNP	Year	Potential GNP
1929	$199.2	1947	$317.3
1930	212.2	1948	324.6
1931	214.8	1949	338.3
1932	214.5	1950	350.6
1933	215.4	1951	364.5
1934	217.9	1952	379.7
1935	222.7	1953	395.8
1936	227.7	1954	412.1
1937	234.0	1955	430.8
1938	241.4	1956	451.5
1939	248.5	1957	472.4
1940	255.6	1958	488.3
1941	263.5	1959	509.0
1942	274.6	1960	523.8
1943	286.7	1961	543.0
1944	300.0	1962	562.4
1945	309.3	1965	622.2
1946	311.9		

[a]Source: For 1929-1960, U.S. Congress, Joint Economic Committee, THE POTENTIAL ECONOMIC GROWTH IN THE UNITED STATES, by James W. Knowles, Joint Committee Print, Study Paper 20 (Washington, D.C.: Government Printing Office, 1960), p. 37. For 1961-1965, U.S. Congress, Joint Economic Committee, "Staff Memorandum on the Relationship of the Federal Budget to Unemployment and to Economic Growth," by James W. Knowles, REPORT OF THE JOINT ECONOMIC COMMITTEE ON THE JANUARY, 1961, ECONOMIC REPORT OF THE PRESIDENT (Washington, D.C.: Government Printing Office, 1961), p. 120.

on a quarterly, constant 1958 dollar basis. For 1968-1970 the average of the four quarters given are used herein. Since no numerical values are given for years prior to 1968, these are approximated by the following formula:

$$o_{t-1} = \frac{o_t}{1 + r}$$

where o_t and o_{t-1} represent potential GNP for a given year and the immediately previous year respectively, and r represents the appropriate trend line growth rate.

Table 6-2
Department of Commerce Estimates of Potential GNP, Annually, 1952-1970 (in billions of 1958 dollars)[a]

Year	Potential GNP	Year	Potential GNP
1952	$395.0	1962	$557.1
1953	408.8	1963	578.0
1954	423.1	1964	599.7
1955	437.9	1965	622.2
1956	453.2	1966	647.1
1957	469.1	1967	673.0
1958	485.5	1968	699.9
1959	502.5	1969	727.9
1960	520.1	1970	758.4
1961	538.3		

[a]Source: See text.

7

Estimation of Potential Output and the Economic Surplus

Selection of the Brookings Study

The Brookings study is used here as the basis for potential output estimates. It was selected in part due to its fame. Its widespread use by economists of various persuasions lends it a great deal of credibility. This is especially true relative to the fascinating but obscure Loeb study. Moreover, since both the Loeb and Brookings studies purport to involve minimum estimates, there is a rough logic involved in selecting the one with the lower estimate. The Brookings study is also a middle-range estimate falling between the estimates of the Loeb study and the Knowles study.

Aside from the credibility-by-fame factor, there is additional ground for selecting the Brookings study in lieu of the later studies. Like so much of the literature of that period of crisis, the Brookings study is very extensive in its scope and method. Its authors surveyed all branches of the economy as to the extent and degree of utilization of capacity. They matched the underemployment of capital with labor availability in translating their findings into aggregate terms.

Later studies are less complete. The estimates by Keyserling and by the Department of Commerce simply apply the sum of productivity and labor force percentage increases to actual output for a given year. Aside from its lack of scope, this procedure implicitly assumes that potential output was attained in the base year. Thus, in computing the aggregate shortfall for 1929-1953, Keyserling uses the actual output of 1929 as representing full potential. This procedure conflicts with the findings of both the Brookings study and the Loeb study that substantial excess aggregate capacity existed in 1929.

The Department of Commerce likewise assumes potential output to have been attained in 1955. Yet Strand and Dernburg estimate gap unemployment rates of 4.03 percent and 4.93 percent for November, 1955, as compared to an official rate of 4.15 percent.[1] Further, the excess capacity studies reviewed in the previous chapter of the present study show excess capacity rates of up to 17 percent for 1955.

The method employed by Knowles to estimate potential output to some extent avoids the simplicity charge. However, it is subject to question as a measure of attainable potential output. Knowles uses a 4 percent unemployment rate in his estimations, assumes actual capacity utilization rates to be optimal, and allows economic obsolescence to limit potential output by incorporating the cyclical demand-shift variable. Further, Knowles' estimates show actual output to have exceeded potential output in 1929. Again, the evidence to the contrary is too great for one to accept the premise that full potential production occurred in 1929.

Selection of Growth Rates

Having selected the Brookings' estimate of potential GNP in 1929 as the basis for estimating potential output, it remains to construct a time series on this base. This involves the selection of a rate of growth, and the selection from the several alternatives is to some extent arbitrary.

One set of alternatives is based upon actual rates of growth. The several possibilities in this set stem from the time period selected. Growth rates prior to 1929 could be used on the basis that prior performance is an appropriate guide as to expected performance. Thus, the average annual rate of growth of Robert Martin's "realized income" for 1900-1929, amounting to 2.7 percent, is a possible choice.[2] So also is the average annual rate of growth of GNP from 1913-1921, which totals 3.1 percent.[3]

Actual growth rates for the 1929-1970 period are also possible choices, since the capacity to produce could be held to change roughly in accord with actual production. Thus, the average annual rates of growth for 1929-1950 of 2.9 percent and for 1950-1970 of 3.6 percent are plausible alternatives.[4] Similarly, the yearly rates of growth of constant dollar GNP are readily computed and must be considered possible alternatives.

Another set of alternatives stems from the growth rates of the potential GNP estimates which are available. The familiar method of summing the percentage changes in productivity per worker and size of the labor force could be employed. Or, the growth rates computed from the potential GNP series of Knowles could be used.

Herein, the annual growth rates of Knowles' potential output estimates are applied to the Brookings' estimate for 1929 to arrive at serial estimates of potential output. These rates were selected by a process of elimination. The rates based upon performance prior to 1929 are significantly lower than actual performance thereafter, except for the Great Depression. Moreover, given the tremendous sociohistorical changes and statistical improvements after 1929, there is no clear warrant for using the rates prior to 1929.

The use of average annual rates, irrespective of the time period upon which they are based or whether actual or potential output is in question, distorts the time distribution of potential output. That is, a rate of growth of 10 percent for one year and 0 percent for nine other years is best presented as such rather than as a 1 percent annual change.

Finally, there is no clear reason for using *actual* growth rates to estimate potential output. Actual growth depends upon the degree of utilization of capacity as well as the volume of capacity. Hence, to use the percent change in actual output as the percent change in potential output would confuse these two very distinct concepts.

Potential Output and the Economic Surplus, 1929-1970

The growth rates used to estimate potential output are given in Table 7-1. For the years 1929-1965, these rates are computed directly from Table 6-1. For 1966-1970, the rates are based on Knowles' middle-range projected rate of growth in potential output. The middle-range rate was selected because it is consistent with Knowles' 1929-1965 series. Knowles projected a 4 percent annual rate of growth in potential from the 1959 potential for the 1959-1975 period.[5]

Table 7-1
Annual Rates of Growth in Knowles' Potential GNP, Annually, 1929-1970[a]

Year	% Rate	Year	% Rate
1930	6.53	1951	3.96
1931	1.23	1952	4.17
1932	−0.14	1953	4.24
1933	0.51	1954	4.12
1934	1.16	1955	4.54
1935	2.20	1956	5.16
1936	2.29	1957	4.63
1937	2.72	1958	3.37
1938	3.16	1959	4.24
1939	2.94	1960	2.91
1940	2.86	1961	3.67
1941	3.09	1962	3.57
1942	4.21	1963	3.43
1943	4.41	1964	3.43
1944	4.64	1965	3.43
1945	3.10	1966	4.00
1946	0.84	1967	4.00
1947	1.73	1968	4.00
1948	2.30	1969	4.00
1949	4.22	1970	4.00
1950	3.64		

[a]Source: Table 6-1.

The potential output estimates for 1929-1970 are given in Table 7-2. These are, of course, derived by applying Table 7-1 growth rates to the Brookings' potential output estimate of $242.5 billion for 1929. For purposes of comparison, actual GNP figures are also presented in Table 7-2 and the ratios of actual to potential GNP in Table 7-3.

Since traditional Marxist surplus income elements do not represent resources available for production, they must be deleted from the output figures. The adjustment process is the same as that used above in Chapter 5 to adjust essential consumption, with one exception, which is that the surplus elements representing surplus industries are not deleted from the output figures because they do

Table 7-2

Potential GNP in the U.S. in Market Prices, Annually, 1929-1970 (in billions of 1958 dollars)[a]

Year	Potential GNP	Actual GNP	Year	Potential GNP	Actual GNP
1929	$242.5	$203.6	1950	$427.5	$355.3
1930	258.3	183.5	1951	444.4	383.4
1931	261.5	169.3	1952	462.9	395.1
1932	261.4	144.2	1953	482.1	412.8
1933	262.7	141.5	1954	502.0	407.0
1934	265.7	154.3	1955	524.8	438.0
1935	271.5	169.5	1956	551.9	446.1
1936	277.7	193.0	1957	577.5	452.5
1937	285.3	203.2	1958	597.0	447.3
1938	294.3	192.9	1959	622.3	475.9
1939	303.0	209.4	1960	640.4	487.7
1940	311.7	227.2	1961	663.9	497.2
1941	321.3	263.7	1962	687.6	529.8
1942	334.8	297.8	1963	711.2	551.0
1943	349.6	337.1	1964	735.6	580.0
1944	365.8	361.3	1965	760.8	614.4
1945	377.1	355.2	1966	791.2	658.1
1946	380.3	312.6	1967	822.8	675.2
1947	386.9	309.9	1968	855.7	706.6
1948	395.8	323.7	1969	889.9	724.7
1949	412.5	324.1	1970	925.5	720.0

[a]Source: Table 7-1; U.S. Department of Commerce, Office of Business Economics, THE NATIONAL INCOME AND PRODUCT ACCOUNTS OF THE UNITED STATES, 1929-1965, STATISTICAL TABLES (Washington, D.C.: Government Printing Office, 1966), pp. 4-5; and SURVEY OF CURRENT BUSINESS, L (July 1970), 17, and LI (July 1971), 13.

Table 7-3
Utilization of Aggregate Capacity, Annually, 1929-1970[a]

Year	Actual÷Potential GNP (in %)	Year	Actual÷Potential GNP (in %)
1929	84.0	1950	83.1
1930	71.0	1951	86.3
1931	64.7	1952	85.4
1932	55.2	1953	85.6
1933	53.9	1954	81.1
1934	58.1	1955	83.5
1935	62.4	1956	80.8
1936	69.5	1957	78.4
1937	71.2	1958	74.9
1938	65.5	1959	76.5
1939	69.1	1960	76.2
1940	72.9	1961	74.9
1941	82.1	1962	77.1
1942	88.9	1963	77.5
1943	96.4	1964	78.8
1944	98.8	1965	80.8
1945	94.2	1966	83.2
1946	82.2	1967	82.1
1947	80.1	1968	82.6
1948	81.8	1969	81.4
1949	78.6	1970	77.8

[a]Derived from Table 7-2.

represent available productive resources. The implications of this process are elaborated fully in Chapter 8. Tables 7-4 and 7-5 summarize the adjustment of the output figures. Table 7-6 contains estimates of the economic surplus for 1929-1970. This table is, of course, the culmination of the empirical aspect of this study.

Table 7-4

Ratio of Surplus Income Elements Imbedded in Market Prices to GNP, Annually, 1929-1970 (in billions of current dollars)[a]

Year	Total	GNP	Ratio	Year	Total	GNP	Ratio
1929	$40.6	$103.1	0.394	1950	$107.1	$284.8	0.376
1930	36.2	90.4	0.400	1951	119.8	328.4	0.365
1931	29.3	75.8	0.387	1952	123.2	345.5	0.357
1932	22.8	58.0	0.393	1953	128.7	364.6	0.353
1933	21.5	55.6	0.387	1954	131.6	364.8	0.361
1934	25.3	65.1	0.389	1955	148.5	398.0	0.373
1935	28.3	72.2	0.392	1956	155.9	419.2	0.372
1936	31.5	82.5	0.382	1957	164.1	441.1	0.372
1937	34.8	90.4	0.385	1958	165.6	447.3	0.370
1938	33.1	84.7	0.391	1959	184.3	483.7	0.381
1939	35.0	90.5	0.387	1960	192.1	503.7	0.381
1940	39.8	100.0	0.398	1961	199.8	520.1	0.384
1941	49.3	124.5	0.396	1962	219.3	560.3	0.391
1942	59.3	157.9	0.376	1963	233.2	590.5	0.395
1943	66.6	191.6	0.348	1964	252.5	631.7	0.400
1944	68.8	210.1	0.327	1965	272.5	681.2	0.400
1945	67.4	211.9	0.318	1966	300.3	749.9	0.400
1946	69.4	208.5	0.333	1967	311.3	793.9	0.392
1947	79.9	231.3	0.345	1968	339.4	864.2	0.393
1948	92.9	257.6	0.361	1969	357.6	929.1	0.385
1949	93.8	256.5	0.357	1970	370.2	974.1	0.380

[a]Source: Tables 5-13 and 5-14.

Table 7-5

GNP After Adjustment for Surplus Income Elements, Annually, 1929-1970 (in billions of 1958 dollars)[a]

Year	Potential	Actual	Year	Potential	Actual
1929	$147.0	$123.4	1950	$266.8	$221.7
1930	155.0	110.1	1951	282.2	243.5
1931	160.3	103.8	1952	297.6	254.0
1932	158.7	87.5	1953	311.9	267.1
1933	161.0	86.7	1954	320.8	260.1
1934	162.3	94.3	1955	329.0	274.6
1935	165.1	103.1	1956	346.6	280.2
1936	171.6	119.3	1957	362.7	284.2
1937	175.5	125.0	1958	376.1	281.8
1938	179.2	117.5	1959	385.2	294.6
1939	185.7	128.4	1960	396.4	301.9
1940	187.6	136.8	1961	409.0	306.3

Table 7-5 (cont.)

Year	Potential	Actual	Year	Potential	Actual
1941	194.1	159.3	1962	418.7	322.6
1942	208.9	185.8	1963	430.3	333.4
1943	227.9	219.8	1964	441.4	348.0
1944	246.2	243.2	1965	456.5	368.6
1945	257.2	242.2	1966	474.7	394.9
1946	253.7	208.5	1967	500.3	410.5
1947	253.4	203.0	1968	519.4	428.9
1948	252.9	206.8	1969	547.3	445.7
1949	265.2	208.4	1970	573.8	446.4

[a]Source: Tables 7-2 and 7-4.

Table 7-6
Economic Surplus, Annually, 1929-1970 (in billions of 1958 dollars)[a]

Year	Potential Surplus	Ratio to Potential Output	Actual Surplus	Ratio to Actual Output	Year	Potential Surplus	Ratio to Potential Output	Actual Surplus	Ratio to Actual Output
1929	$ 56.9	0.387	$ 33.3	0.270	1950	$149.1	0.559	$104.0	0.469
1930	65.1	0.420	20.2	0.183	1951	157.1	0.557	118.4	0.486
1931	67.9	0.424	11.4	0.110	1952	162.2	0.545	118.6	0.467
1932	67.7	0.427	−3.5	−0.040	1953	168.0	0.539	123.2	0.461
1933	71.2	0.442	−3.1	−0.036	1954	171.7	0.535	111.0	0.427
1934	74.4	0.458	6.4	0.068	1955	175.9	0.535	121.5	0.442
1935	76.4	0.463	14.4	0.140	1956	188.0	0.542	121.6	0.434
1936	77.9	0.454	25.6	0.215	1957	200.0	0.551	121.5	0.428
1937	79.5	0.453	29.0	0.232	1958	207.2	0.551	112.9	0.401
1938	81.9	0.457	20.2	0.172	1959	213.4	0.554	122.8	0.417
1939	83.2	0.448	25.9	0.202	1960	217.6	0.549	123.1	0.408
1940	87.4	0.466	36.6	0.268	1961	224.1	0.548	121.4	0.396
1941	96.6	0.498	61.8	0.388	1962	229.4	0.548	137.7	0.427
1942	103.8	0.497	80.7	0.434	1963	235.3	0.547	138.4	0.415
1943	121.6	0.534	113.5	0.516	1964	241.1	0.546	147.7	0.424
1944	137.4	0.558	134.4	0.553	1965	250.5	0.549	162.6	0.441
1945	148.3	0.577	133.3	0.550	1966	262.6	0.553	182.8	0.463
1946	149.4	0.589	104.2	0.500	1967	282.9	0.565	193.1	0.470
1947	146.3	0.577	95.9	0.472	1968	293.4	0.565	202.9	0.473
1948	144.0	0.569	97.9	0.473	1969	313.9	0.574	212.3	0.476
1949	150.5	0.567	93.7	0.450	1970	336.6	0.587	209.2	0.469

[a]Source: Tables 5-15 and 7-5. It should be noted that the column Potential Surplus contains the surplus concept that is employed throughout this paper. The actual surplus is presented here solely for the reader's convenience for comparison purposes. The actual surplus differs from this potential surplus only to the extent of the gap between potential and actual output. That is, essential consumption rather than actual consumption is the consumption concept used.

8

The Economic Surplus and Neo-Marxism: Comparison and Conclusions

Methodological Summary

Before comparing the foregoing to a number of neo-Marxist hypotheses, it seems advisable to summarize the method of this study. Emphasis is placed upon the product side of the national accounts ledger. The economic surplus is defined as potential output minus total essential consumption, the latter being the sum of personal essential consumption, essential social overhead consumption, and essential capital consumption. The elements comprising the economic surplus are nonessential personal, social overhead, and capital consumption; social and private investment; the output of surplus industries; and the gap between actual and potential output.

The first step toward estimation of the economic surplus is the estimation of total essential consumption. The data for this estimation are supplied in Chapters 4 and 5 as summarized in terms of current market prices in Table 5-10. These serial estimates of total essential consumption are then adjusted to exclude surplus elements imbedded in market prices. These adjustments are summarized in Tables 5-11 to 5-15.

The surplus elements within market prices are of two types. Type one contains surplus income elements: profits, government revenues, rent, and interest. Type two contains the output of surplus industries: advertising, finance, insurance, and real estate.[a] For the adjustment of total essential consumption, the type one and type two surplus elements are summed, and their ratio to GNP for the respective years is used to make the adjustment.

Estimates of potential output and data on actual output are supplied in Chapters 6 and 7, culminating in Table 7-2, which presents both in terms of market prices. Here the question of adjusting these output series arises and with it the significance of the distinction between type one and type two surplus elements in the structure of market prices. The type two elements represent resources that could be used to produce (socially useful) output other (rather) than the sales effort and other middling activities. On the other hand, the type one elements are solely of income distributive interest. They do not represent

---

[a]Since surplus income elements are included in the type one category, only wages and salaries of surplus industries are used in the type two category. There are some minor discrepancies involved, such as capital and social overhead consumption in the surplus industries.

productive resources that could be used to alter the size or composition of total output.[b]

This last may draw opposition. Such opposition would probably stem from an emotional reaction to visions of an impoverished peasantry or proletariat relative to an idle *rentier* or to industrial/financial captains wheeling and dealing in pecuniary dramas. Certainly such social types represent unused output potential. However, the number of those purely idle is probably very small in relative terms and would therefore have little impact on potential output estimates. As for those not idle but engaged in nonproductive pecuniary activities, the approach must center on their potential productivity not on the actual income they receive.

To use personal income as an estimate of output potential for either the purely or pecuniarily-involved idle, one must assume that the market or other device evaluates the incomes of idleness in terms of output potential. One would be hard-pressed to argue that stock dividends or executive salaries are correlated to the potential productivities of their recipients.

This is not meant to imply that Marxists would argue such a point. Rather, their concern with regard to the surplus generally rests not with unproduced potential output but with unnecessary produced output, the latter being consumed by nonproducers and therefore unnecessary. So long as the market operates along the lines of the purely competitive model, the incomes of unnecessary factors correspond to surplus output. However, to the extent that there exists unutilized output potential other than the property income recipients, or to the extent that the competitive law of value is not supreme in the determination of incomes and output composition, this correspondence fails.

Thus the correspondence between personal property incomes and surplus output has been weakened. The control once vested with property incomes has been institutionalized in large corporate and financial institutions, and to these institutions must turn the search for the surplus. The important surplus institution is no longer the super-rich magnate but the surplus economic sectors such as advertising, finance, and other paper-shuffling activities.[c]

The upshot of all this is that property incomes and government revenues are best treated as transfers. Thus, they are to be deleted from both output and essential consumption prior to subtracting for the economic surplus. Thus, whereas essential consumption is adjusted for both types of surplus elements in market prices, output is adjusted only for the type one elements.[d]

---

[b]There could of course occur an indirect change in the size or composition of output given some shift in the distribution of income. However, due to the definition of personal essential consumption used, this phenomenon is not important here.

[c]The author is reminded of the scene in the movie entitled *Joe* in which blue-collar Joe, viewing the multistory office building, queries the business executive as to the content of his work. The executive replies, "We move paper."

[d]The type one adjustment is made because the surplus income elements would otherwise effect the serial distribution of the surplus.

If the above is correct, an identical surplus should be derivable from the income side of the ledger by using procedures consistent with the output surplus concept. The crucial linkage is that of necessary income that unsurprisingly equals total essential consumption. That is, essential income is income necessary to purchase essential consumption. Thus, the income surplus would be the sum of personal disposable income minus personal essential consumption, government revenue minus essential social overhead, nominal capital consumption minus essential capital consumption, and the potential/actual output gap.

This, of course, yields surplus personal income that does not correspond to the output surplus, the difference being transfers. Property incomes are viewed as transfer payments also. That is, minimum consumption is viewed as a necessary social cost. The income necessary to purchase this output, where not provided as a necessary cost of production, is provided via transfer payments, which may be effected by government fiscal mechanisms or by property income claims. Hence, to achieve the factor income surplus, i.e., that which corresponds to the output surplus, the adjustment for surplus income elements would need to be made.

Monopoly Capitalism

Before comparing the findings of the current study with a number of neo-Marxist hypotheses, it is necessary to briefly compare the concepts and methods of the current study with those of the classic neo-Marxist study.[1] The basic difference between the present approach and that of Baran and Sweezy is the reluctance of the latter to suspend the primary role of the market and its law of value.

Overall, monopoly capitalism is as unplanned as its competitive predecessor. The big corporations relate to each other [and to others] primarily through the market. . . . And since market relations are essentially price relations, the study of monopoly capitalism, like that of competitive capitalism, must begin with the workings of the price mechanism.[2]

What is of concern here is how this view affects Baran and Sweezy's approach to the economic surplus.[3] Baran and Sweezy use the same point of departure as is used in the current study. Early on they regard the surplus as "the difference between what a society produces and the costs of producing it."[4] Moreover, Baran in an earlier book alludes to essential consumption for capitalists and to essential social consumption.[5] All this points to the total essential consumption definition employed in the current study. The essential consumption of *all* persons in society is a necessary charge on society's output. Likewise, essential governmentally supplied goods and services constitute such a charge.

Yet Baran and Sweezy relegate all property incomes and all government expenditures to the economic surplus. As explained in Chapter 3 above, this treatment of government is inexplicable. The treatment of property incomes follows from their approximation of the surplus as the difference between national income and the wages of productive workers, i.e., as property incomes.[6] Thus, they continue to view labor as exchanging for its cost of production. That is, they continue to apply the law of value of competitive capitalism.

However, Baran and Sweezy partially recognize the inoperability of the law of value. Advertising and other such activities should be minimized in a competitive situation. Otherwise, since they cannot cut into the subsistence of the productive class, they cut into the unearned incomes of the dominant class. Why then have these activities grown so in the era of monopoly capitalism? Precisely because the law of value is not operative. Wages are not equal to subsistence, nor do the prices of property goods represent necessary ransom prices for the owners of these goods.

Ultimately, Baran and Sweezy pierce themselves upon this thorn by *adding* property incomes and nonessential output. The confusion and intermingling of the two sides of the national accounts is traceable to their desire to have the surplus represent two different magnitudes, unearned incomes and nonessential output.[7]

This quandary is avoided in the present study by defining the surplus as the difference between potential output and the share thereof necessary to reproduce the extant productive capacity. The law of value is not assumed to be operative.[8] Thus, no *a priori* case exists for equating costs of production with the wages of labor nor for equating surplus with property incomes.

The Neo-Marxist Hypotheses

Of the various speculations, theorems, and tendencies set forth by Baran and Sweezy concerning the laws of motion of monopoly capitalism, three are of central importance. These are, one, that the surplus rises over time both absolutely and as a percentage of national income; two, that the investment-seeking portion of the surplus rises over time as a percentage of the surplus; and, three, that monopoly capitalism is incapable of absorbing this rising investment-seeking portion. The importance of these three hypotheses derives from their being the line of reasoning upon which Baran and Sweezy conclude that monopoly capitalism is inherently stagnationist and unable to supply the quality of life one can rightfully expect from so much potential abundance.

Each of these hypotheses is considered in turn *vis-à-vis* the evidence of the current study. In the process, the differences between the current approach and that of Baran and Sweezy are elaborated more fully. Also, the basis is established for the conclusions drawn in the final section of the study.

The Rising Surplus

Baran and Sweezy state that "there is a strong and systematic tendency for [the] surplus to rise, both absolutely and as a share of total output." Although formulated under the "first approximation" of the surplus as being equal to aggregate profits, the clear implication is that this "law" applies to more complex definitions of the surplus as well.[9]

A brief glance at Table 7-6 shows that the surplus as herein defined and estimated corroborates this thesis in both its absolute and relative dimensions. However, little should be made of this since the thesis itself is uninteresting under the definition of the surplus herein employed. Baran and Sweezy in the context of this hypothesis are obviously emphasizing the distributive shares as between earned and unearned income aspect of the surplus. Here, of course, the surplus is not viewed in this context. Viewed in the context of the difference between potential output and essential output, the rising surplus merely implies that technological change is increasing potential output faster than essential consumption is increasing.

Parenthetically, there are at least two issues which might make the hypothesis interesting. First, the rising surplus could be taken to imply increasing returns in the aggregate. However, one hardly needs so elaborate a technique to demonstrate the existence of technical change. Moreover, if one confines the returns to scale concept to a given technology, the surplus concept is not applicable.

The rising surplus could also be taken to be a measure of the elasticity of essential consumption relative to rising potential output. That is, the rising surplus relative to output implies that a variant of Engel's Law applies to essential consumption. Since essential consumption is subject to secular evolution upward, this question is not *a priori* determined. However, this does not suffice to make the question interesting on an ordinal scale of alternative research questions.

Also parenthetically, the defining away of the relative shares aspect of the surplus should not be interpreted as denying the importance either of the surplus in the analysis of class relations nor of the degree of inequality of income distribution. The dominant class still appropriates the surplus to its own ends. That is, the surplus is still used in a manner that protects the vested positions of power and prestige in the *status quo*. Moreover, the distribution of income remains clearly relevant in this distribution of power and prestige. The current analysis simply separates these two important sets of questions rather than lumping them together as the surplus. On the one hand, the surplus measures the amount of output whose use involves a large element of social choice. On the other hand, the question of the distribution of income and power concerns the manner in which this choice is made and the participants who dominate in this process.

*The Rising Investment-Seeking Portion
of the Surplus*

The second of the neo-Marxist hypotheses under consideration maintains that
the investment-seeking portion of the surplus tends to rise. Baran and Sweezy
make an *a fortiori* case for this tendency based on the pattern of dividend
distribution in the modern corporation. They reason that since the dividend
policies of these corporations cause a lag between the accumulation of the rising
surplus and the distribution of this surplus into disposable income, then even *if*
the capitalists spend all distributed profits on consumption, the investment-
seeking share of the surplus will rise.[10]

This *a fortiori* case fails under the present definition of the surplus. That is,
since nonessential consumption can be other than that of the capitalist class, it is
possible that this other consumption will offset the lack of increased capitalists'
consumption relative to the total surplus.

It is possible, however, to perform a relatively simple test of the hypothesis.
The difference between potential output and the sum of personal and social
consumption can be safely construed as the investment-seeking portion of the
surplus. It should be noted that the element of the surplus absorbed by surplus
industries or nonessential social consumption is not considered in the argument
at this point. Baran and Sweezy consider these elements after having demonstrated the rising investment-seeking portion as a first approximation.[11]

Table 8-1 contains serial data on total personal consumption and essential
social consumption. The personal consumption series is, of course, adjusted for
surplus elements imbedded in market prices before being summed with the social
consumption series. Table 8-1 also shows the investment-seeking portion of the
surplus and its ratio to the total surplus.

The evidence could hardly be more damaging to the neo-Marxist thesis. The
ratio of the investment-seeking portion of the surplus to the total surplus has
demonstrated a marked tendency to decline since 1929. Indeed, up to World
War II, the investment-seeking share exceeded the (potential) surplus. This
means, in effect, that a significant share of the population had a level of living
below the essential consumption standard.

The social implication of this negation is that the New Deal coalition and the
neo-Keynesian ethic that have held sway in U.S. politics since the Depression
have indeed altered the face of capitalism. The increases in social overhead
consumption[e] and the bolstering of private consumption have altered the
investment/consumption balance.

---

[e]It should be noted that defense spending and the waste of surplus industries remain in the
investment-seeking share to this point.

Table 8-1

The Investment-Seeking Portion of the Surplus, Annually, 1929-1970 (in billions of 1958 dollars)[a]

Year	Potential Output	Consumption	Investment-Seeking	Economic Surplus	Ratio
1929	$147.0	$ 87.1	$ 59.9	$ 56.9	1.053
1930	155.0	81.0	74.0	65.1	1.137
1931	160.3	79.4	80.9	67.9	1.191
1932	158.7	70.8	87.9	67.7	1.298
1933	161.0	70.7	90.3	71.2	1.268
1934	162.3	74.3	88.0	74.4	1.182
1935	165.1	78.7	86.4	76.4	1.131
1936	171.6	88.8	82.8	77.9	1.063
1937	175.5	91.3	84.2	79.5	1.059
1938	179.2	89.0	90.2	81.9	1.101
1939	185.7	94.1	91.6	83.2	1.101
1940	187.6	97.0	90.6	87.4	1.037
1941	194.1	103.8	90.3	96.6	0.935
1942	208.9	106.0	102.9	103.8	0.991
1943	227.9	113.5	114.4	121.6	0.941
1944	246.2	120.6	125.6	137.4	0.914
1945	257.2	129.3	127.9	148.3	0.862
1946	253.7	141.5	112.2	149.4	0.751
1947	253.4	142.3	111.1	146.3	0.759
1948	252.9	144.5	108.4	144.0	0.753
1949	265.2	149.0	116.2	150.5	0.772
1950	266.8	155.7	111.1	149.1	0.745
1951	282.2	161.7	120.5	157.1	0.767
1952	297.6	170.6	127.0	162.2	0.783
1953	311.9	179.1	132.8	168.0	0.790
1954	320.8	180.4	140.4	171.7	0.818
1955	329.0	188.9	140.1	175.9	0.796
1956	346.6	196.1	150.5	188.0	0.801
1957	362.7	202.5	160.2	200.0	0.801
1958	376.1	207.1	169.0	207.2	0.816
1959	385.2	214.8	170.4	213.4	0.799
1960	396.4	223.0	173.4	217.6	0.797
1961	409.0	228.2	180.8	224.1	0.807
1962	418.7	236.7	182.0	229.4	0.793
1963	430.3	246.7	183.6	235.3	0.780

Table 8-1 (cont.)

Year	Potential Output	Consumption	Investment-Seeking	Economic Surplus	Ratio
1964	441.4	260.0	181.4	241.1	0.752
1965	456.5	276.1	180.4	250.5	0.720
1966	474.7	294.7	180.0	262.6	0.685
1967	500.3	311.6	188.7	282.9	0.667
1968	519.4	329.8	189.6	293.4	0.646
1969	547.3	350.9	196.4	313.9	0.627
1970	573.8	364.8	209.0	336.6	0.621

aSource: Tables 5-10, 5-14, and 7-5; U.S. Department of Commerce, Office of Business Economics, THE NATIONAL INCOME AND PRODUCT ACCOUNTS OF THE UNITED STATES, 1929-1965, STATISTICAL TABLES (Washington, D.C.: Government Printing Office, 1966), pp. 4-5; and SURVEY OF CURRENT BUSINESS, L (July 1970), 17, and LI (July 1971), 13.

The Declining Operating Rate of Total Capacity

The final hypothesis to be considered concerns the degree of utilization of productive capacity. Specifically, it is held that the investment-seeking share of the surplus cannot be absorbed. Therefore, "the *normal* state of the monopoly capitalist economy is stagnation." Further, the operating rate of capacity will drift downward over time.[12] The authors do admit of offsetting tendencies such as militarization and waste. But, however much they bemoan the meteoric rise of these superfluous activities, the clear implication of the discussion is that these elements cannot rise apace with the capacity to produce.[13]

The test of this hypothesis is easily performed. The ratio of actual GNP to potential GNP is clearly a measure of the aggregate utilization of capacity. Such a ratio is given in seriatim in Table 7-3. Since there has been no persistent downward trend in the utilization rate, the hypothesis is apparently contradicted.

There are, however, a number of qualifications upon this conclusion. Most of these are discussed in a different context by Baran and Sweezy. They discuss the New Deal and the possibility that it has reached its limit and the defense revolution its possible upper limit.[14] The argument is that these elements may have reached the limit of their capacity to protect monopoly capitalism from stagnation.

A less speculative qualification is contained in the data itself. The peak operating rates of capacity appear to be trending slightly downward. Coupled with the fact that the trough operating tables are trending upward, this implies that the increase in stability may have been purchased at the expense of a stable stagnation.[15] At any rate, and despite these qualifications, the operating rate of capacity appears unlikely to engender revolutionary fervor in the moderately distant future.

Conclusions and Recommendations

Throughout this study, particularly in the empirical estimation sections, the author has expressed his lack of complete satisfaction with some of the techniques and concepts employed. Such expressions are obviously recommendations for further research. Thus, for example, in the areas of measuring depreciation, depletion, and social overhead consumption, the author suggests the inadequacy of the current state of affairs.

With these in mind, this concluding section can be restricted to the major conceptual implications of the study. These, of course, relate to the body of literature consistently referred to as neo-Marxism. The fundamental theme of these implications is that Baran and Sweezy, in their reformulation of Marxism, are moving in a direction pregnant with potential for important social analysis. Their view of the modern corporation as the institutionalized capitalist and of the importance of waste in monopoly capitalism are examples of such movement. However, in these and other cases, Baran and Sweezy fail to travel far enough. They continue to analyze the class situation primarily in terms of classical Marxism's Moneybags and the subsistence-living proletariat. Hence, they fail to entertain the possible scenario of power-wielding technocrats and overfed workers.[16] This latter scenario is at the heart of most recent radical social analysis that is steeped in the heritage of the young Marx.[17]

Thus, Baran and Sweezy fail to escape the traditional Marxist emphasis on *quantitative* cycles and secular stagnation of national output. They imply that limits exist upon the surplus absorption power of militarism and waste despite empirical evidence to the contrary. This leaves them precariously close to the traditional Marxist notion that unemployment and material impoverishment will eventually goad the proletariat into revolution.

To be an effective instrument of social analysis and change, neo-Marxism must give up this emphasis on quantitative aggregates. It must be recognized that the capitalist engine is not going to throttle itself in a crisis of underproduction and underutilization of capacity.

We do not predict that there will be any automatic breakdown of capitalism, but rather assert that it will end through revolutionary struggles (as determined *in part* by the economic conditions). ... *If* capitalism were static and purely competitive ..., *then* maybe there would be a long-run trend to underconsumption, worse and worse depression, and/or eventual stagnation. [However,] there is no observable trend to worse depressions since the 1930s. ...[18]

Rather, the crisis is to be based upon qualitative foundations. It must be based upon a growing awareness of waste and irrationality that causes a lack of faith in the institutions of society and a displacement of those who man these institutions.

There are two important subsidiary implications of the above: the allocation problem must again become the paramount economic problem and the supersession of the market mechanism must be admitted. The neo-Marxist concern with the degree of waste in monopoly capitalism attests to the importance of the allocation question. So also does the increased degree of choice due to the widening range between output and necessary consumption.

However, in Marxist economics since its birth and in mainstream economics since the Keynesian Revolution, the major concern of political economy has been the level of aggregate employment and output, not the composition of such. Nevertheless, current techniques in this field seem more or less adequate for the task. That is, the technical capability exists through a bevy of monetary/fiscal mechanisms to maintain a chosen level of output. What is retarded are the techniques for choosing that level and its composition.[19]

Moreover, even to the extent that the techniques of demand policy fail versus their dilemma of "stagflation" and resort is made to wage/price policy, the problem is allocative in nature. For in the process of employing wage/price controls to secure acceptable aggregate results, the basis for any argument as to allocation via the invisible hand is destroyed. That is, if public policy is to assume the role of determining the degree of flexibility of prices, it must also assume responsibility for the allocation decisions such flexibility is supposed to determine.

This latter point makes it imperative that social analysis begin with the question of power rather than market/price relations as do Baran and Sweezy. It must be recognized that monopoly capitalism is *not* so unplanned as its predecessor. That quite to the contrary, there exists extensive planning.[20] However much one wishes to distinguish democratic socialist planning from elitist or technostructural planning, denying the existence of the latter is an inappropriate tactic.

The fact of planning is clearly true in relation to the quantitative level of output. There is no doubt that the broad outlines of Galbraith's "management of specific demand" and "regulation of aggregate demand" are a reality.[21] Further, the data of the current study show a narrowing of the gaps between the peaks of expansion and the troughs of contraction and deny any marked quantitatively stagnationist tendencies.

The gist of the argument is that the market system should no longer be viewed as an impersonal allocator of resources. Rather, the market should be viewed as an instrument of planning.

. . . Technically, but only technically, the market mechanism still allocates resources to uses. [The underlying reality] can be understood best by reference to an example of a planned economy—where the planning authority relies on the market mechanism to allocate resources, but where, also, it substitutes its own preferences for those of the consumer. . . . Suppose now that instead of a public planning authority we are dealing with a huge corporation in private hands that owns (directly or indirectly) all productive units in the economy. Such a super-monopolist has no less power [than would the planning authority]. . . .

With this interpretation, Galbraith's argument—that in the modern industrial state planning is superseding the market—has an important and revealing meaning. . . .

What is remarkable is that this valuable insight into the workings of contemporary capitalism is shared by so few.[22]

The import to which Papandreou alludes is simply that planning is a fact of life. The quality of modern society, be it nominally socialist or capitalist, hinges not on planning versus nonplanning, but on who plans, on what is planned, and on how the who plans the what. Galbraith sees the planning as technocratic and Papandreou as paternalistic. In both cases planning is elitist, and in both cases, many factors of human welfare are being omitted from the planning matrix.

Thus, the problem reduces to one of control. Since power is inherently personal,[23] the question may be asked in terms of who controls the market and the other instruments of planning, and what institutionalized process holds them accountable for using their power toward appropriate ends. This is an allocation problem as well as a political problem. Since allocation is no longer primarily effected via the market, much of what passes in economics as the theory of allocation is irrelevant. A share of the income/control equation becomes irrelevant in this fashion. The one-to-one correspondence between income and market votes need not apply in the relation between income and political votes. Therefore, neo-Marxism must investigate the possibility that the technocrat rather than Moneybags is dominant in the makeup of the dominant class.

Bibliography

Bibliography

Books

Baran, Paul A. THE POLITICAL ECONOMY OF GROWTH. New York: Monthly Review Press, 1957.

_____ , and Sweezy, Paul M. MONOPOLY CAPITAL: AN ESSAY ON THE AMERICAN ECONOMIC AND SOCIAL ORDER. New York: Monthly Review Press, 1966.

Bator, Francis M. THE QUESTION OF GOVERNMENT SPENDING: PUBLIC NEEDS AND PRIVATE WANTS. New York: Harper and Brothers, 1960.

Bell, Daniel, and Kristol, Irving, eds. CAPITALISM TODAY. New York: Basic Books, 1970, 1971.

Berle, A.A. POWER. New York: Harcourt, Brace, and World, 1967.

Blaug, Mark. ECONOMIC THEORY IN RETROSPECT. Revised ed. Homewood, Ill.: Richard D. Irwin, Inc., 1968.

Carver, Thomas Nixon. PRINCIPLES OF NATIONAL ECONOMY. Boston: Ginn and Co., 1921.

Childe, V. Gordon. WHAT HAPPENED IN HISTORY?. Baltimore: Penguin Books, 1946.

_____ . SOCIAL EVOLUTION. London: Watts and Company, 1951.

Comish, Newell H. THE STANDARD OF LIVING: ELEMENTS OF CONSUMP-TION. New York: Macmillan Company, 1923.

Committee for Economic Development. FURTHER WEAPONS AGAINST INFLATION: MEASURES TO SUPPORT GENERAL FISCAL AND MONE-TARY POLICIES. New York: Committee for Economic Development, 1970.

Creamer, Daniel. CAPITAL EXPANSION AND CAPACITY IN POST-WAR MANUFACTURING. New York: National Industrial Conference Board, Inc., 1961.

Creamer, Daniel. RECENT CHANGES IN MANUFACTURING CAPACITY. New York: National Industrial Conference Board, Inc., 1962.

Dearing, Charles L. AMERICAN HIGHWAY POLICY. Washington, D.C.: Brookings Institution, 1941.

Engels, Frederick. THE ORIGIN OF THE FAMILY, PRIVATE PROPERTY, AND THE STATE. SELECTED WORKS: IN ONE VOLUME. In Karl Marx and Frederick Engels. New York: International Publishers, 1968.

Friedman, Milton. CAPITALISM AND FREEDOM. Chicago: University of Chicago Press, 1962.

Galbraith, John Kenneth. THE AFFLUENT SOCIETY. Boston: Houghton-Mifflin Company, 1958.

_____ . THE NEW INDUSTRIAL STATE. Boston: Houghton-Mifflin Company, 1967.

Harrington, Michael. THE ACCIDENTAL CENTURY. Baltimore: Penguin Books, Inc., 1966.

_____. TOWARD A DEMOCRATIC LEFT. Baltimore: Penguin Books, Inc., 1968.

Hebden, Norman, and Smith, Wilbur S. STATE-CITY RELATIONSHIPS IN HIGHWAY AFFAIRS. New Haven: Yale University Press, 1950.

Keynes, John Maynard. THE GENERAL THEORY OF EMPLOYMENT, IN-TEREST, AND MONEY. Harbinger ed. New York: Harcourt, Brace, and World, Inc., 1964.

Keyserling, Leon H. TOWARD FULL EMPLOYMENT AND FULL PRODUC-TION: HOW TO END OUR NATIONAL ECONOMIC DEFECTS. Washington, D.C.: Conference on Economic Progress, 1954.

_____. TWO TOP-PRIORITY PROGRAMS TO REDUCE UNEMPLOY-MENT. Washington, D.C.: Conference on Economic Progress, 1963.

_____. PROGRESS OR POVERTY. Washington, D.C.: Conference on Economic Progress, 1964.

_____. AGRICULTURE AND THE PUBLIC INTEREST: TOWARD A NEW FARM PROGRAM. Washington, D.C.: Conference on Economic Progress, 1965.

Kiker, B.F. HUMAN CAPITAL: IN RETROSPECT. Columbia, S.C.: Bureau of Business and Economic Research, 1968.

Kolko, Gabriel. WEALTH AND POWER IN AMERICA. New York: Praeger Publishers, 1962.

Leven, Maurice; Moulton, Harold G.; and Warburton, Clark. AMERICA'S CAPACITY TO CONSUME. Washington, D.C.: Brookings Institution, 1934.

Marshall, Alfred. PRINCIPLES OF ECONOMICS. 9th (Variorum) ed., Vol. I. New York: Macmillan Company, 1961.

Martin, Robert F. NATIONAL INCOME IN THE UNITED STATES, 1799-1938. New York: National Industrial Conference Board, 1939.

Marx, Karl. CAPITAL: A CRITIQUE OF POLITICAL ECONOMY. 3 vols. New York: International Publishers, 1967.

Meier, Richard L. SCIENCE AND ECONOMIC DEVELOPMENT: NEW PAT-TERNS OF LIVING. 2nd ed. Cambridge, Mass.: MIT Press, 1956.

Miliband, Ralph. THE STATE IN CAPITALIST SOCIETY. New York: Basic Books, 1969.

Moulton, Harold G. THE FORMATION OF CAPITAL. Washington, D.C.: Brookings Institution, 1935.

_____. INCOME AND ECONOMIC PROGRESS. Washington, D.C.: Brookings Institution, 1935.

Musgrave, Richard A. THE THEORY OF PUBLIC FINANCE: A STUDY IN PUBLIC ECONOMY. New York: McGraw-Hill Book Co., 1959.

National Bureau of Economic Research. Vol. XI of STUDIES IN INCOME AND WEALTH. New York: National Bureau of Economic Research, 1949.

_____. Vol XV of STUDIES IN INCOME AND WEALTH. New York: National Bureau of Economic Research, 1952.

_____. A CRITIQUE OF THE UNITED STATES INCOME AND PRODUCT ACCOUNTS. Vol. XXII of STUDIES IN INCOME AND WEALTH. Princeton, N.J.: Princeton University Press, 1958.

Nourse, Edwin G., and Associates. AMERICA'S CAPACITY TO PRODUCE. Washington, D.C.: Brookings Institution, 1934.

Papandreou, Andreas G. PATERNALISTIC CAPITALISM. Minneapolis: University of Minnesota Press, 1972.

Pipping, Hugo E. STANDARD OF LIVING: THE CONCEPT AND ITS PLACE IN ECONOMICS. Helsingfors, Finland: SOCIETAS SCIENTARIUM FENNICA, 1953.

Reagan, Michael D. THE MANAGED ECONOMY. New York: Oxford University Press, 1963.

Robinson, Joan. FREEDOM AND NECESSITY: AN INTRODUCTION TO THE STUDY OF SOCIETY. New York: Vintage Books, 1971.

Sherman, Howard. RADICAL POLITICAL ECONOMY: CAPITALISM AND SOCIALISM FROM A MARXIST HUMANIST PERSPECTIVE. New York: Basic Books, 1972.

Shonfield, Andrew. MODERN CAPITALISM: THE CHANGING BALANCE OF PUBLIC AND PRIVATE POWER. New York: Oxford University Press, 1965.

Smith, Robert S., and de Vyver, Frank, eds. ECONOMIC SYSTEMS AND PUBLIC POLICY: ESSAYS IN HONOR OF CALVIN B. HOOVER. Durham, North Carolina: Duke University Press, 1966.

Spencer, Milton H. CONTEMPORARY ECONOMICS. New York: Worth Publishers, Inc., 1971.

Steindl, J. MATURITY AND STAGNATION IN AMERICAN CAPITALISM. Oxford: Basil Blackwell, 1952.

Strachey, John. CONTEMPORARY CAPITALISM. New York: Random House, 1956.

Streever, Donald C. CAPACITY UTILIZATION AND BUSINESS INVESTMENT. Urbana, Ill.: University of Illinois Bureau of Economic and Business Research, 1960.

Sweezy, Paul M. THE THEORY OF CAPITALIST DEVELOPMENT: PRINCIPLES OF MARXIAN POLITICAL ECONOMY. New York: Monthly Review Press, 1942 and 1968.

Theobald, Robert, ed. SOCIAL POLICIES FOR AMERICA IN THE SEVENTIES: NINE DIVERGENT VIEWS. New York: Doubleday and Company, Inc., 1968.

Veblen, Thorstein. THE THEORY OF THE BUSINESS ENTERPRISE. New York: Charles Scribner's Sons, 1904.

_____. THE VESTED INTERESTS AND THE STATE OF THE INDUSTRIAL ARTS. New York: B.W. Heubsch, 1919.

Veblen, Thorstein. THE ENGINEERS AND THE PRICE SYSTEM. Harbinger ed. New York: Harcourt, Brace, and World, 1963.

Wilson, George W., ed. CLASSICS OF ECONOMIC THEORY. Bloomington, Inc.: Indiana University Press, 1964.

Articles

Allen, Clark Lee. "Economic Freedom and Public Policy." ECONOMIC SYSTEMS AND PUBLIC POLICY: ESSAYS IN HONOR OF CALVIN B. HOOVER. Edited by Robert S. Smith and Frank de Vyver. Durham, North Carolina: Duke University Press, 1966.

"Alternative Estimates of Corporate Depreciation and Profits, 1965-70." SURVEY OF CURRENT BUSINESS, LII (January 1972), 34-35.

Barloon, Marvin. "The Question of Steel Capacity." HARVARD BUSINESS REVIEW, XXVII (March 1949), 209-236.

Beach, E.F. "A Measurement of the Productive Capacity of Wealth." CANADIAN JOURNAL OF ECONOMICS AND POLITICAL SCIENCE, VII (November 1941), 538-544.

Bernard, L.L. "Standards and Planes of Living." SOCIAL FORCES, VII (1928-1929), 115-126.

Bourneuf, Alice. "Manufacturing Investment, Excess Capacity, and the Rate of Growth of Output." AMERICAN ECONOMIC REVIEW, LIV (September 1964), 607-625.

Brackett, Jean C. "New BLS Budgets Provide Yardsticks for Measuring Family Living Costs." MONTHLY LABOR REVIEW, XCII (April 1969), 3-16.

Brandis, Royall. "Obsolescence and Investment." JOURNAL OF ECONOMIC ISSUES, I (September 1967), 169-187.

Budd, Edward C. "Treatment of Distributive Shares." National Bureau of Economic Research, A CRITIQUE OF THE UNITED STATES INCOME AND PRODUCT ACCOUNTS, Vol. XXII. Princeton, N.J.: Princeton University Press, 1958.

Butler, William F. "Capacity Utilization and the Rate of Profitability in Manufacturing." AMERICAN ECONOMIC REVIEW/SUPPLEMENT, XLVIII (May 1958), 239-248.

Davis, J.S. "Standards and Content of Living." AMERICAN ECONOMIC REVIEW, XXXV (March 1945), 1-15.

Denison, Edward F. "Income Types and the Size Distribution." AMERICAN ECONOMIC REVIEW/SUPPLEMENT, XLIV (May 1954), 254-269.

Eisner, Robert. "Depreciation Allowances, Replacement Requirements, and Growth." AMERICAN ECONOMIC REVIEW, XLII (December 1952), 820-831.

_____. "Depreciation Under the New Tax Law." HARVARD BUSINESS REVIEW, XXXIII (January-February 1955), 66-74.

"Estimated Intercity Differences in Cost of Living, June 15, 1939." MONTHLY LABOR REVIEW, L (November 1939), 1164-1167.

"Estimated Intercity Differences in Cost of Living, December 15, 1939." MONTHLY LABOR REVIEW, LI (April 1940), 923-925.

"Estimated Intercity Differences in Cost of Living, June 15, 1942." MONTHLY LABOR REVIEW, LV (September 1942), 570-573.

"Estimated Intercity Differences in Cost of Living, March 15, 1943." MONTHLY LABOR REVIEW, LVII (October 1943), 803-805.

Fisher, Franklin M., Griliches, Zvi; and Kaysen, Carl. "The Costs of Automobile Model Changes Since 1949." JOURNAL OF POLITICAL ECONOMY, LXX (October 1962), 433-451.

Fletcher, Max E. "Liberal and Conservative: Turn and Turnabout." JOURNAL OF ECONOMIC ISSUES, II (September 1968), 312-322.

Frankel, Marvin. "Obsolescence and Technical Change in a Maturing Economy." AMERICAN ECONOMIC REVIEW, XLV (June 1955), 296-319.

Golanskii, M. "Methods Employed to Recalculate the National Income of the U.S.A." PROBLEMS OF ECONOMICS, II (March 1960), 57-63.

Groom, Phyllis. "A New City Workers' Family Budget." MONTHLY LABOR REVIEW, XC (November 1967), 1-8.

"Intercity Differences in Cost of Living, December, 1942." MONTHLY LABOR REVIEW, LVI (April 1943), 745-747.

Keyserling, Leon H. "The Problem of Problems: Economic Growth." SOCIAL POLICIES FOR AMERICA IN THE SEVENTIES: NINE DIVERGENT VIEWS. Edited by Robert Theobald. New York: Doubleday and Company, Inc., 1968.

Kiker, B.F. "The Historical Roots of the Concept of Human Capital." JOURNAL OF POLITICAL ECONOMY, LXXIV (October 1966), 481-499.

Knapp, Eunice M. "City Workers' Family Budget for October, 1951." MONTHLY LABOR REVIEW, LXVI (May 1952), 520-522.

Koffsky, Nathan. "Farm and Urban Purchasing Power." National Bureau of Economic Research, STUDIES IN INCOME AND WEALTH, Vol. XI. New York: National Bureau of Economic Research, 1949.

Lamale, Helen H. "Changes in Concepts of Income Adequacy Over the Last Century." AMERICAN ECONOMIC REVIEW/SUPPLEMENT, XLVII (May 1958), 291-299.

_____, and Stotz, Margaret S. "The Interim City Workers' Family Budget." MONTHLY LABOR REVIEW, LXXXIII (August 1960), 785-808.

Lubitz, Raymond. "Monopoly Capitalism and Neo-Marxism." CAPITALISM TODAY. Edited by Daniel Bell and Irving Kristol. New York: Basic Books, 1970, 1971.

Magdoff, Harry. "The Purpose and Method of Measuring Productivity." JOURNAL OF THE AMERICAN STATISTICS ASSOCIATION, XXXIV (June 1939), 309-318.

Meeker, Royal. "What is the American Standard of Living?" MONTHLY LABOR REVIEW, IX (July 1919), 1-13.

Orshansky, Mollie. "Equivalent Levels of Living: Farm and City." National Bureau of Economic Research, STUDIES IN INCOME AND WEALTH, Vol. XIV. New York: National Bureau of Economic Research, 1952.

_____. "Children of the Poor." SOCIAL SECURITY BULLETIN, XXVI (July 1963), 3-13.

_____. "Counting the Poor: Another Look at the Poverty Profile." SOCIAL SECURITY BULLETIN, XXVIII (Jaunary 1965), 3-29.

_____. "Who's Who Among the Poor: A Demographic View of Poverty." SOCIAL SECURITY BULLETIN, XXVIII (July 1965), 3-32.

Peixotto, Jessica B. "Family Budgets." AMERICAN ECONOMIC REVIEW/SUPPLEMENT, XVII (March 1927), 132-140.

Robb, Lewis H. "Industrial Capacity and Its Utilization." SCIENCE AND SOCIETY, XVII (fall 1953), 318-325.

Ruiz, Elizabeth. "Spring 1970 Cost Estimates for Urban Family Budgets." MONTHLY LABOR REVIEW, XCIV (January 1971), 59-62.

Samuelson, Paul A. "Aspects of Public Expenditure Theories." REVIEW OF ECONOMICS AND STATISTICS, XL, No. 4 (1958), 332-338.

Schultz, Theodore W. "Investment in Human Capital." AMERICAN ECONOMIC REVIEW, LI (March 1961), 1-17.

Staehle, Hans. "Annual Survey of Statistical Information: Family Budgets." ECONOMETRICA, II and III (October, 1934, and January, 1935), 349-362 and 106-118.

Stanfield, J.R. "Veblen's 'Revolutionary Overturn' and THE NEW INDUSTRIAL STATE." REVIEW OF SOCIAL THEORY, I (September 1972), 12-18.

Strand, Kenneth, and Dernburg, Thomas. "Cyclical Variation in Civilian Labor Force Participation." REVIEW OF ECONOMICS AND STATISTICS, XLVI (November 1964), 378-391.

Ulin, Robert P. "Are We Building Too Much Capacity?" HARVARD BUSINESS REVIEW, XXXIII (November-December 1955), 41-47.

Weisskopf, Thomas E. "The Problem of Surplus Absorption in a Capitalist Society." THE CAPITALIST SYSTEM. Edited by Richard C. Edwards, Michael Reich, and Thomas E. Weisskopf. Englewood Cliffs, New Jersey: Prentice-Hall, Inc., 1972.

Williams, Faith M. "Living Costs in 1938." MONTHLY LABOR REVIEW, XLVIII (March 1939), 531-537.

Young, Allan H. "Alternative Estimates of Corporate Depreciation and Profits: Parts I and II." SURVEY OF CURRENT BUSINESS, XLVIII (April 1968), 17-28, and (May 1968), 16-28.

Government Documents

U.S. Congress. Joint Economic Committee. THE POTENTIAL ECONOMIC GROWTH IN THE UNITED STATES, by James W. Knowles. Joint Committee Print, Study Paper 20. Washington, D.C.: Government Printing Office, 1960.

U.S. Congress. Joint Economic Committee. REPORT OF THE JOINT ECONOMIC COMMITTEE ON THE JANUARY 1961 ECONOMIC REPORT OF THE PRESIDENT. 87th Cong., 1st sess., 1961.

U.S. Congress. Senate. Committee on Government Operations. FULL OPPORTUNITY AND SOCIAL ACCOUNTING ACT. HEARINGS before a subcommittee on Government Research of the Committee on Government Operations, Senate, on S. 843, Part 2, 90th Cong., 1st sess., 1967.

U.S. Department of Commerce. Bureau of the Census. CURRENT POPULATION REPORTS, Series P-20, nos. 26 and 33, POPULATION CHARACTERISTICS. Washington, D.C.: Government Printing Office, 1950 and 1951.

U.S. Department of Commerce. Bureau of the Census. CURRENT POPULATION REPORTS, Series P-20, nos. 106, 164, 173, and 191, HOUSEHOLD AND FAMILY CHARACTERISTICS. Washington, D.C.: Government Printing Office, 1961, 1967, 1968, and 1969.

U.S. Department of Commerce. Bureau of the Census. STATISTICAL ABSTRACT OF THE UNITED STATES, 1971 EDITION. Washington, D.C.: Government Printing Office, 1971.

U.S. Department of Commerce. Office of Business Economics. UNITED STATES INCOME AND OUTPUT. Washington, D.C.: Government Printing Office, 1958.

U.S. Department of Commerce. Office of Business Economics. THE NATIONAL INCOME AND PRODUCT ACCOUNTS OF THE UNITED STATES, 1929-1965, STATISTICAL TABLES. Washington, D.C.: Government Printing Office, 1966.

U.S. Department of Labor. Bureau of Labor Statistics. HANDBOOK OF LABOR STATISTICS, 1941 Edition, Bull. 694. Washington, D.C.: Government Printing Office, 1941.

U.S. Department of Labor. Bureau of Labor Statistics. CHANGES IN COST OF LIVING IN LARGE CITIES IN THE UNITED STATES, 1913-1941, Bull. 699. Washington, D.C.: Government Printing Office, 1941.

U.S. Department of Labor. Bureau of Labor Statistics. WORKER'S BUDGETS IN THE UNITED STATES: CITY FAMILIES AND SINGLE PERSONS, 1946 and 1947, Bull. 927. Washington, D.C.: Government Printing Office, 1948.

U.S. Department of Labor. Bureau of Labor Statistics. HANDBOOK OF

LABOR STATISTICS, 1950 EDITION, Bull. 1016. Washington, D.C.: Government Printing Office, 1950.

U.S. Department of Labor. Bureau of Labor Statistics. CITY WORKERS' FAMILY BUDGET: FOR A MODERATE LIVING STANDARD, AUTUMN, 1966, Bull. 1570-1. Washington, D.C.: Government Printing Office, 1967.

U.S. Department of Labor. Bureau of Labor Statistics. REVISED EQUIVA-LENCE SCALE: FOR ESTIMATING EQUIVALENT INCOMES OR BUD-GET COSTS BY FAMILY TYPE, Bull. 1570-2. Washington, D.C.: Government Pringing Office, 1968.

U.S. Department of Labor. Bureau of Labor Statistics. 3 STANDARDS OF LIVINGS: FOR AN URBAN FAMILY OF FOUR PERSONS, Bull. 1570-5. Washington, D.C.: Government Printing Office, 1969.

U.S. Department of Labor. Bureau of Labor Statistics. THREE BUDGETS: FOR A RETIRED COUPLE IN URBAN AREAS OF THE UNITED STATES, 1967-1968, Bull. 1570-6. Washington, D.C.: Government Printing Office, 1970.

U.S. Treasury Department. Internal Revenue Service. Bulletin F (Revised January 1942). INCOME TAX, DEPRECIATION, AND OBSOLESCENCE, ESTIMATED USEFUL LIVES AND DEPRECIATION RATES. Washington, D.C.: Government Printing Office, 1942.

U.S. Works Progress Administration. Division of Social Research. QUANTITY BUDGETS FOR BASIC MAINTENANCE AND EMERGENCY STAND-ARDS OF LIVING, by Margaret L. Stecker, Research Bulletin, Series I, no. 21. Washington, D.C.: Government Printing Office, 1936.

U.S. Works Progress Administration. Division of Social Research. INTERCITY DIFFERENCES IN COSTS OF LIVING IN MARCH, 1935, 59 CITIES, Research Monograph 12. Washington, D.C.: Government Printing Office, 1937.

Miscellany

Bills, Sharyn, Staff Associate, Division of Hospital Public Relations, American Hospital Association. Personal letter. April 4, 1972.

Bureau of Applied Economics, Inc. STANDARDS OF LIVING: A COM-PILATION OF BUDGET STUDIES. Revised ed. Bulletin no. 7. Washington, D.C.: Bureau of Applied Economics, Inc., 1921.

Johnson, Harry G. "Economics and Everyday Life." Lecture delivered at the annual banquet of Omicron Delta Epsilon, Oklahoma Alpha Chapter, Nor-man, Oklahoma, April 21, 1972.

Kloster, Linda, Information Services, Air Transport Association. Personal letter. March 10, 1972.

Loeb, Harold, Director. REPORT OF THE NATIONAL SURVEY OF POTEN-

TIAL PRODUCT CAPACITY. New York: New York City Housing Authority, 1935.

National Industrial Conference Board. FAMILY BUDGETS OF AMERICAN WAGE-EARNERS: A CRITICAL ANALYSIS. Research Report no. 21. New York: The Century Co., 1921.

Notes

Notes

Chapter 1
The Economic Surplus

1. Paul A. Baran and Paul M. Sweezy, MONOPOLY CAPITAL: AN ESSAY ON THE AMERICAN ECONOMIC AND SOCIAL ORDER (New York: Monthly Review Press, 1966).

2. Thomas E. Weisskopf, "The Problem of Surplus Absorption in a Capitalist Society," in THE CAPITALIST SYSTEM, edited by Richard C. Edwards, Michael Reich, and Thomas E. Weisskopf (Englewood Cliffs, New Jersey: Prentice-Hall, Inc., 1972), p. 366. The distinction between necessary and surplus production is beautifully illustrated by Joan Robinson, FREEDOM AND NECESSITY: AN INTRODUCTION TO THE STUDY OF SOCIETY (New York: Vintage Books, 1971).

3. See, for example, V. Gordon Childe, WHAT HAPPENED IN HISTORY? (Baltimore: Penguin Books, 1946) and SOCIAL EVOLUTION (London: Watts and Company, 1951).

4. Marvin Harris, "The Economy Has No Surplus?," AMERICAN ANTHROPOLOGIST, LXI (April 1959), 185.

5. George W. Wilson, "An Essay on the History of Economic Thought," in CLASSICS OF ECONOMIC THEORY, edited by George W. Wilson (Bloomington, Indiana: Indiana University Press, 1964), pp. 9-36.

6. Weisskopf, "The Problem of Surplus Absorption in a Capitalist Society," p. 366.

7. Paul A. Baran, THE POLITICAL ECONOMY OF GROWTH (New York: Monthly Review Press, 1957), p. 23 and 23n. (Italics in original).

8. Ibid., p. 33.

9. Baran and Sweezy, MONOPOLY CAPITAL, p. 9.

10. Joseph D. Phillips, "Estimating the Economic Surplus," in ibid., Appendix, p. 369.

11. Ibid., pp. 370-384.

Chapter 2
Definition of Personal Essential Consumption

1. David Ricardo, "Principles of Political Economy and Taxation," in CLASSICS OF ECONOMIC THEORY, edited by George W. Wilson (Bloomington: Indiana University Press, 1964), p. 275.

2. Karl Marx, CAPITAL: A CRITIQUE OF POLITICAL ECONOMY, Vol. 1 (New York: International Publishers, 1967), pp. 170-171.

3. Ricardo, "Principles of Political Economy and Taxation," p. 276.

4. Ibid., p. 277.

5. Marx, CAPITAL, Vol. I, p. 171.

6. Paul A. Baran, THE POLITICAL ECONOMY OF GROWTH (New York: Monthly Review Press, 1957, 1968), p. xvi.

7. Marx, CAPITAL, Vol. I, p. 171.

8. Baran, THE POLITICAL ECONOMY OF GROWTH, p. 30.

9. It is convenient to note here the distinction between a "standard" and a "level." The level (or plane or scale) relates to an *actual* quantity of consumption or some other entity. The standard relates to a norm or abstract quantity, whether empirically or ideally derived. See L.L. Bernard, "Standards and Planes of Living," SOCIAL FORCES, VII (1928-1929), 115ff, or J.S. Davis, "Standards and Content of Living," AMERICAN ECONOMIC REVIEW, XXXV (March 1945), 2-3 and 7-8.

10. Hugo E. Pipping, STANDARD OF LIVING: THE CONCEPT AND ITS PLACE IN ECONOMICS (Helsingfors, Finland: SOCIETAS SCIENTARIUM FENNICA, 1953), pp. 126ff.

11. Richard L. Meier, SCIENCE AND ECONOMIC DEVELOPMENT: NEW PATTERNS OF LIVING (2nd ed.; Cambridge, Mass.: MIT Press, 1956), p. 162.

12. See for example Meier's argument, ibid., pp. 156-176.

13. Pipping, STANDARD OF LIVING, pp. 127-128.

14. Thomas Nixon Carver, PRINCIPLES OF NATIONAL ECONOMY (Boston: GINN and Co., 1921), p. 579.

15. Helen H. Lamale, "Changes in Concepts of Income Adequacy Over the Last Century," AMERICAN ECONOMIC REVIEW/SUPPLEMENT, XLVII (May 1958), 292. The research on the Continent by Frederick Le Play and E. Ducpetiaux, and their student Ernst Engel is no doubt to be expected from Ms. Lamale's survey. See U.S. Department of Labor, Bureau of Labor Statistics, WORKERS' BUDGETS IN THE U.S.: CITY FAMILIES AND SINGLE PERSONS, 1946 and 1947, "Family Budgets: A Historical Survey," by Dorothy S. Brady, Bulletin 927 (Washington, D.C.: Government Printing Office, 1948), pp. 41-42.

16. For surveys, see National Industrial Conference Board, FAMILY BUDGETS OF AMERICAN WAGE-EARNERS: A CRITICAL ANALYSIS, Research Report No. 21 (New York: The Century Co., 1921), pp. 1-50. Bureau of Applied Economics, Inc., STANDARDS OF LIVING: A COMPILATION OF BUDGET STUDIES, revised edition, Bulletin No. 7 (Washington, D.C., 1921). Hans Staehle, "Annual Survey of Statistical Information: Family Budgets," ECONOMETRICA, II and III (October 1934, and January 1935), 349-362 and 106-118, respectively.

17. This brief historical discussion relies in the main upon the references listed in Footnote 15, this chapter.

18. For a detailed summary of several nationwide and local studies in the

1900-1929 period, see the National Industrial Conference Board's Research Report cited in Footnote 16, this chapter. The survey by Staehle, cited in the same footnote, contains a number of budget studies for countries other than the U.S.

19. U.S. Works Progress Administration, Division of Social Research, INTER-CITY DIFFERENCES IN COSTS OF LIVING IN MARCH, 1935, 59 CITIES (Washington, D.C.: Government Printing Office, 1937), p. xiii. The budget is given in detail in U.S. Works Progress Administration, Division of Social Research, QUANTITY BUDGETS FOR BASIC MAINTENANCE AND EMERGENCY STANDARDS OF LIVING, by Margaret L. Stecker, Research Bulletin Series I, No. 21 (Washington, D.C.: Government Printing Office, 1936).

20. U.S. Works Progress Administration, Division of Social Research, INTER-CITY DIFFERENCES IN COSTS OF LIVING, pp. xiii-xiv.

21. U.S. Department of Labor, Bureau of Labor Statistics, Workers' Budgets in the U.S.: . . . , 1946 and 1947, p. 3.

22. Ibid., pp. 1, 3, 4, 9, passim.

23. Helen H. Lamale and Margaret S. Stotz, "The Interim City Workers' Family Budget," MONTHLY LABOR REVIEW, LXXXIII (August 1960), 785-791.

24. Phyllis Groom, "A New City Workers' Family Budget," ibid., XC (November 1967), 1-8.

25. Jean C. Brackett, "New BLS Budgets Provide Yardsticks for Measuring Family Living Costs," ibid., XCII (April 1969), 3, 5, and 7.

26. Mollie Orshansky, "Counting the Poor: Another Look at the Poverty Profile," SOCIAL SECURITY BULLETIN, XXVIII (January, 1965), 5-6 and 7-9. See also other references to Ms. Orshansky's work listed in the bibliography.

27. Orshansky, "Counting the Poor," 10-11.

28. U.S. Department of Labor, Bureau of Labor Statistics, WORKERS' BUDGETS IN THE U.S.: . . . , 1946 and 1947, p. 3.

29. Ibid., p. 4.

30. Ibid., p. 6.

31. Ibid., p. 7.

Chapter 3
Definition of Social Essential Consumption

1. John Kenneth Galbraith, THE AFFLUENT SOCIETY (Boston: Houghton-Mifflin, Co., 1958), Chapter 8.

2. For an extended discussion of proportionality, as among the different lines of production and as between aggregate production and consumption, which is based upon and includes extensive bibliographic references to the works of Marx and later Marxists, see Paul M. Sweezy, THE THEORY OF CAPITAL-

IST DEVELOPMENT: PRINCIPLES OF MARXIAN POLITICAL ECONOMY (New York: Monthly Review Press, 1942 and 1968), Chapter 10.

3. Adam Smith, "An Inquiry into the Nature and Causes of the Wealth of Nations," in CLASSICS OF ECONOMIC THEORY, edited by George W. Wilson (Bloomington: Indiana University Press, 1964), pp. 149-158.

4. Ibid., p. 153.

5. John Stuart Mill, "Principles of Political Economy," in CLASSICS OF ECONOMIC THEORY, edited by Wilson, pp. 374-378.

6. Alfred Marshall, PRINCIPLES OF ECONOMICS (9th variorum ed.; New York: Macmillan Co., 1961), Vol. I, pp. 443n-444n and 717-718.

7. See Paul A. Samuelson, "Aspects of Public Expenditure Theories," REVIEW OF ECONOMICS AND STATISTICS, XL, no. 4 (1958), p. 332.

8. See Mark Blaug, ECONOMIC THEORY IN RETROSPECT (revised ed.; Homewood, Illinois: Richard D. Irwin, Inc., 1968), pp. 368-373 and 381-396.

9. Milton Friedman, CAPITALISM AND FREEDOM (Chicago: University of Chicago Press, 1962), Chapter 2.

10. Richard A. Musgrave, THE THEORY OF PUBLIC FINANCE: A STUDY IN PUBLIC ECONOMY (New York: McGraw-Hill Book Co., 1959), Chapter 1.

11. These developments are dealt with in numerous places. For example, in addition to the major works of Galbraith, Baran, and Sweezy, see Michael D. Reagan, THE MANAGED ECONOMY (New York: Oxford University Press, 1963); Andrew Shonfield, MODERN CAPITALISM: THE CHANGING BAL-ANCE OF PUBLIC AND PRIVATE POWER (New York: Oxford University Press, 1965); Clark Lee Allen, "Economic Freedom and Public Policy," in ECONOMIC SYSTEMS AND PUBLIC POLICY: ESSAYS IN HONOR OF CALVIN B. HOOVER, edited by Robert S. Smith and Frank T. de Vyver (Durham, North Carolina: Duke University Press, 1966), pp. 3-18; Max E. Fletcher, "Liberal and Conservative: Turn and Turnabout," JOURNAL OF ECONOMIC ISSUES, II (September 1968), 312-322.

12. Frederick Engels, THE ORIGIN OF THE FAMILY, PRIVATE PROPER-TY, AND THE STATE, in SELECTED WORKS: IN ONE VOLUME, by Karl Marx and Frederick Engels (New York: International Publishers, 1968).

13. See Sweezy, THEORY OF CAPITALIST DEVELOPMENT, Chapter 13.

14. Karl Marx, CAPITAL, Vol. I (New York: International Publishers, 1967), Part 3, Chapter 10.

15. John Strachey, CONTEMPORARY CAPITALISM (New York: Random House, 1956).

16. Ralph Miliband, THE STATE IN CAPITALIST SOCIETY (New York: Basic Books, 1969), Chapter 4 and passim.

17. Sweezy, THEORY OF CAPITALIST DEVELOPMENT, Chapter 13.

18. Paul A. Baran and Paul M. Sweezy, MONOPOLY CAPITAL: AN ESSAY ON THE AMERICAN ECONOMIC AND SOCIAL ORDER (New York: Monthly Review Press, 1966), Chapter 6.

19. Paul A. Baran, THE POLITICAL ECONOMY OF GROWTH (New York: Monthly Review Press, 1957), pp. 23n and 92ff.

20. Theodore W. Schultz, "Investment in Human Capital," AMERICAN ECONOMIC REVIEW, LI (March 1961), 1-5.

21. These distinctions arise, however involutely, in the review works by B.F. Kiker, "The Historical Roots of the Concept of Human Capital," JOURNAL OF POLITICAL ECONOMY, LXXIV (October 1966), 481-499, and HUMAN CAPITAL: IN RETROSPECT (Columbia, South Carolina: Bureau of Business and Economic Research, 1968).

22. U.S. Department of Labor, Bureau of Labor Statistics, 3 STANDARDS OF LIVING: FOR AN URBAN FAMILY OF FOUR PERSONS, Bulletin 1570-5 (Washington, D.C.: Government Printing Office, 1968), p. 65.

23. Marx, CAPITAL, Vol. I, pp. 203 and 207.

24. Ibid., p. 203.

25. Royall Brandis, "Obsolescence and Investment," JOURNAL OF ECONOMIC ISSUES, I (September 1967), 169-172.

26. J. Steindl, MATURITY AND STAGNATION IN AMERICAN CAPITALISM (Oxford: Basil Blackwell, 1952), pp. 4-14. See also the classic, but still highly useful, unintentional indictment of the anarchism of capitalist production in the four-volume Brookings Institution study. Edwin G. Nourse and Associates, AMERICA'S CAPACITY TO PRODUCE (Washington, D.C.: Brookings Institution, 1934); Maurice Leven, Harold G. Moulton, and Clark Warburton, AMERICA'S CAPACITY TO CONSUME (Washington, D.C.: Brookings Institution, 1934); Harold G. Moulton, INCOME AND ECONOMIC PROGRESS (Washington, D.C.: Brookings Institution, 1935); and Harold G. Moulton, THE FORMATION OF CAPITAL (Washington, D.C.: Brookings Institution, 1935).

27. Marvin Frankel, "Obsolescence and Technical Change," AMERICAN ECONOMIC REVIEW, XLV (June 1955), 299ff.

28. See Baran and Sweezy, MONOPOLY CAPITAL, pp. 99-100.

29. M. Golanskii, "Methods Employed to Recalculate the National Income of the U.S.A.," PROBLEMS OF ECONOMICS, II (March 1960), 57-63.

30. These problems are variously discussed in the literature. See, for example, the following: Robert Eisner, "Depreciation Allowances, Replacement Requirements, and Growth," AMERICAN ECONOMIC REVIEW, XLII (December 1952), 820 and 831, and "Depreciation Under the New Tax Law," HARVARD BUSINESS REVIEW, XXXIII (January-February 1955), 66-74; National Bureau of Economic Research, A CRITIQUE OF THE U.S. INCOME AND PRODUCT ACCOUNTS, STUDIES IN INCOME AND WEALTH, Vol. XXII (Princeton, N.J.: Princeton University Press, 1958), especially 77-80, 85-91, 252-263, and 431-447; and U.S. Department of Commerce, Office of Business Economics, U.S. INCOME AND OUTPUT (Washington, D.C.: Government Printing Office, 1958), pp. 115ff.

31. Allan H. Young, "Alternative Estimates of Corporate Depreciation and

Profits: Parts I and II," SURVEY OF CURRENT BUSINESS, XLVIII (April 1968), 17-28, and (May 1968), 16-28.

32. Eisner, "Depreciation Allowances, Replacement Requirements and Growth," pp. 820 and 831, challenges the traditional view that the use of original cost is a distortion.

33. Young, "Alternative Estimates of Corporate Depreciation and Profits: Parts I and II."

34. U.S. Treasury Department, Internal Revenue Service, Bulletin F (revised January 1942), INCOME TAX, DEPRECIATION, AND OBSOLESCENCE, ESTIMATED USEFUL LIVES AND DEPRECIATION RATES (Washington, D.C.: Government Printing Office, 1942).

35. Young, "Alternative Estimates of Corporate Depreciation and Profits: Parts I and II," Part II, pp. 18-19.

36. For cogent literature on the problems of treating depletion allowances, see the various authors in National Bureau of Economic Research, A CRITIQUE OF THE UNITED STATES INCOME AND PRODUCT ACCOUNTS, especially pp. 93-94, 264-266, and 487-504.

Chapter 4
Estimation of Personal Essential Consumption

1. For the reasons for this choice, see Chapter 2, above.

2. Phyllis Groom, "A New City Workers' Family Budget," MONTHLY LABOR REVIEW, XC (November 1967), 1-2.

3. See U.S. Department of Labor, Bureau of Labor Statistics, CITY WORKERS' FAMILY BUDGET: FOR A MODERATE LIVING STANDARD, AUTUMN, 1966, Bulletin 1570-1 (Washington, D.C.: Government Printing Office, 1967), p. 9. Jean C. Brackett, "New BLS Budgets Provide Yardsticks for Measuring Family Living Costs," MONTHLY LABOR REVIEW, XCII (April 1969), 8. Elizabeth Ruiz, "Spring 1970 Cost Estimates for Urban Family Budgets," ibid., XCIV (January 1971), 60.

4. U.S. Department of Labor, Bureau of Labor Statistics, WORKERS' BUDGETS IN THE UNITED STATES: CITY FAMILIES AND SINGLE PER-SONS, 1946 AND 1947, Bulletin 927 (Washington, D.C.: Government Printing Office, 1948), p. 40.

5. Helen H. Lamale and Margaret S. Stotz, "The Interim City Workers' Family Budget," MONTHLY LABOR REVIEW, LXXXIII (August 1960), 801.

6. U.S. Department of Labor, Bureau of Labor Statistics, WORKERS' BUDGETS IN THE UNITED STATES: . . . , 1946 AND 1947, p. 40.

7. Lamale and Stotz, "The Interim City Workers' Family Budget," p. 787.

8. U.S. Department of Labor, Bureau of Labor Statistics, CITY WORKERS' FAMILY BUDGET: . . . , AUTUMN 1966, p. 9. U.S. Department of Labor,

Bureau of Labor Statistics, 3 STANDARDS OF LIVING FOR AN URBAN FAMILY OF FOUR, Bulletin 1570-5 (Washington, D.C.: Government Printing Office, 1969), p. 15.

9. See U.S. Department of Labor, Bureau of Labor Statistics, HANDBOOK OF LABOR STATISTICS, 1950 EDITION Bulletin 1016 (Washington, D.C.: Government Printing Office, 1950), p. 122n.

10. Jean C. Brackett, "New BLS Budgets Provide Yardsticks for Measuring Family Living Costs," MONTHLY LABOR REVIEW, XCII (April 1969), 16.

11. U.S. Department of Labor, Bureau of Labor Statistics, HANDBOOK OF LABOR STATISTICS, 1941 EDITION, Bulletin 694 (Washington, D.C.: Government Printing Office, 1941), p. 99.

12. U.S. Department of Labor, Bureau of Labor Statistics, HANDBOOK OF LABOR STATISTICS, 1950 EDITION, p. 100.

13. As a test, the 981 CPI for the year 1935 and the 139.5 CPI for 1946 were used with the respective budget costs to derive an adjustment factor by the same method. These figures yield a factor of 1.4896, which is judged not significantly different.

14. See Newell H. Comish, THE STANDARD OF LIVING: ELEMENTS OF CONSUMPTION (New York: Macmillan Co., 1923), p. 76, or Royall Meeker, "What is the American Standard of Living?," MONTHLY LABOR REVIEW, IX (July 1919), 5.

15. Comish, THE STANDARD OF LIVING, p. 76.

16. U.S. Department of Labor, Bureau of Labor Statistics, HANDBOOK OF LABOR STATISTICS, 1950 EDITION, p. 121. For method, see U.S. Department of Labor, Bureau of Labor Statistics, Workers' Budgets in the United States: . . . , 1946 and 1947, pp. 50-51.

17. Gabriel Kolko, WEALTH AND POWER IN AMERICA (New York: Praeger Publishers, 1962), p. 157, n. 6.

18. U.S. Department of Labor, Bureau of Labor Statistics, WORKERS' BUDGETS IN THE UNITED STATES: . . . , 1946 AND 1947, p. 51.

19. Lamale and Stotz, "Interim City Workers' Family Budget," 789-790.

20. U.S. Department of Labor, Bureau of Labor Statistics, REVISED EQUIVALENCE SCALE: FOR ESTIMATING EQUIVALENT INCOMES OR BUDGET COSTS BY FAMILY TYPE, Bulletin 1570-2 (Washington, D.C.: Government Printing Office, 1968), pp. 14ff. The scales for elderly families are presented in a separate publication. U.S. Department of Labor, Bureau of Labor Statistics, THREE BUDGETS: FOR A RETIRED COUPLE IN URBAN AREAS OF THE UNITED STATES, 1967-1968, Bulletin 1570-6 (Washington, D.C.: Government Printing Office, 1970).

21. See Mollie Orshansky, "Children of the Poor," SOCIAL SECURITY BULLETIN, XXVI (July 1963), p. 313, and "Counting the Poor: Another Look at the Poverty Profile," SOCIAL SECURITY BULLETIN, XXVIII (January 1965), pp. 14-17.

22. Orshansky, "Counting the Poor," p. 9.

23. U.S. Department of Labor, Bureau of Labor Statistics, REVISED EQUIVALENCE SCALE, p. 14.

24. See Orshansky, "Counting the Poor," 9-10, and "Who's Who Among the Poor: A Demographic View of Poverty," SOCIAL SECURITY BULLETIN, XXVII (July 1965), 9-10.

25. See Nathan Koffsky, "Farm and Urban Purchasing Power," National Bureau of Economic Research, STUDIES IN INCOME AND WEALTH, Vol. XI (New York: National Bureau of Economic Research, 1949), pp. 155-156, 172, and passim.

26. Ibid., p. 154.

27. See especially his discussions of clothing, p. 163, and housing, p. 167.

28. See U.S. Department of Commerce, Bureau of the Census, CURRENT POPULATION REPORTS, Series P-20, no. 191, HOUSEHOLD AND FAMILY CHARACTERISTICS: MARCH, 1968, (Washington, D.C.: Government Printing Office, 1969), p. 4.

Chapter 5
Estimation of Social Essential Consumption

1. It should be remembered that the natural resources item is included here for convenience. See Chapter 3.

2. Francis M. Bator, THE QUESTION OF GOVERNMENT SPENDING: PUBLIC NEEDS AND PRIVATE WANTS (New York: Harper and Brothers, 1960), p. 138.

3. Charles L. Dearing, AMERICAN HIGHWAY POLICY (Washington, D.C.: Brookings Institution, 1941), pp. 113-114.

4. Norman Hebden and Wilbur S. Smith, STATE-CITY RELATIONSHIPS IN HIGHWAY AFFAIRS (New Haven: Yale University Press, 1950), pp. 11-12, 12n.

5. Personal letter from Ms. Linda Kloster, Information Services, Air Transport Association, dated March 10, 1972.

6. Milton H. Spencer, CONTEMPORARY ECONOMICS (New York: Worth Publishers, Inc., 1971), back fly page.

7. The figure for 1940 is used in lieu of the unavailable 1930 figure.

8. Personal letter from Ms. Sharyn Bills, Staff Associate, Division of Hospital Public Relations, American Hospital Association, April 4, 1972.

9. U.S. Department of Commerce, Bureau of the Census, STATISTICAL ABSTRACT OF THE UNITED STATES, 1971 (Washington, D.C.: Government Printing Office, 1971), pp. 5 and 70.

10. Allan H. Young, "Alternative Estimates of Corporate Depreciation and Profits: Parts I and II," SURVEY OF CURRENT BUSINESS, XLVIII (April 1968), 17-28, and (May 1968), 16-28.

Chapter 6
Excess Capacity, Unemployment, and Potential Output

1. Examples of the underworld treatment of these elements are easy to find. See: Thorstein Veblen, THE THEORY OF THE BUSINESS ENTERPRISE (New York: Charles Scribner's Sons, 1904), and THE VESTED INTERESTS AND THE STATE OF THE INDUSTRIAL ARTS (New York: B.W. Huebsch, 1919), especially Chapter 4, "Free Income." Harold Loeb, Director, REPORT OF THE NATIONAL SURVEY OF POTENTIAL PRODUCT CAPACITY (New York: New York City Housing Authority, 1935), especially pp. xiv-xxiii and 207-247. Paul A. Baran, THE POLITICAL ECONOMY OF GROWTH (New York: Monthly Review Press, 1957), pp. 34-39. Paul A. Baran and Paul M. Sweezy, MONOPOLY CAPITAL: AN ESSAY ON THE AMERICAN ECONOMIC AND SOCIAL ORDER (New York: Monthly Review Press, 1966), Ch. 5. An exception to the neglect of this area by orthodox economists that demonstrates the type of research needed is Franklin M. Fisher, Zvi Griliches, and Carl Kaysen, "The Costs of Automobile Model Changes Since 1949," JOURNAL OF POLITICAL ECONOMY, LXX (October 1962), 433-451.

2. John Maynard Keynes, THE GENERAL THEORY OF EMPLOYMENT, INTEREST, AND MONEY (Harbinger ed.; New York: Harcourt Brace and World, Inc., 1964), p. 379.

3. Loeb, REPORT OF THE NATIONAL SURVEY OF POTENTIAL PRODUCT CAPACITY, pp. xiv-xv.

4. Ibid., p. xv.

5. Veblen, VESTED INTERESTS AND THE STATE OF THE INDUSTRIAL ARTS, p. 81.

6. Loeb, REPORT OF THE NATIONAL SURVEY OF POTENTIAL PRODUCT CAPACITY, pp. xvi-xvii.

7. Ibid., p. xvii.

8. Edwin G. Nourse and Associates, AMERICA'S CAPACITY TO PRODUCE (Washington, D.C.: Brookings Institution, 1934), pp. 21-28.

9. Donald C. Streever, CAPACITY UTILIZATION AND BUSINESS INVESTMENT (Urbana, Illinois: University of Illinois Bureau of Economic and Business Research, 1960), pp. 24-25.

10. Daniel Creamer, CAPITAL EXPANSION AND CAPACITY IN POST-WAR MANUFACTURING (New York: National Industrial Conference Board, Inc., 1961), p. 19.

11. Ibid., p. 18.

12. Nourse, AMERICA'S CAPACITY TO PRODUCE, pp. 144, 301, and 307.

13. Streever, CAPACITY UTILIZATION AND BUSINESS INVESTMENT, p. 64.

14. Ibid., p. 64.

15. Baran and Sweezy, MONOPOLY CAPITAL, pp. 237 and 242.

16. Lewis H. Robb, "Industrial Capacity and Its Utilization," SCIENCE AND SOCIETY, XVII (Fall 1953), 319-324.

17. Creamer, CAPITAL EXPANSION AND CAPACITY IN POSTWAR MANUFACTURING, p. 25.

18. Daniel Creamer, RECENT CHANGES IN MANUFACTURING CAPACITY (New York: National Industrial Conference Board, Inc., 1962), Table A-6.

19. Robert P. Ulin, "Are We Building Too Much Capacity?" HARVARD BUSINESS REVIEW, XXXIII (November-December 1955), 42.

20. William F. Butler, "Capacity Utilization and the Rate of Profitability in Manufacturing," AMERICAN ECONOMIC REVIEW/SUPPLEMENT, XLVIII (May 1958), 241.

21. Baran and Sweezy, MONOPOLY CAPITAL, p. 247.

22. Alice Bourneuf, "Manufacturing Investment, Excess Capacity, and the Rate of Growth of Output," AMERICAN ECONOMIC REVIEW, LIV (September 1964), 622.

23. See J. Steindl, MATURITY AND STAGNATION IN AMERICAN CAPITALISM (Oxford, England: Basil Blackwell, 1952), pp. 4-14, for a theoretical discussion thereon.

24. Ulin, "Are We Building Too Much Capacity?" p. 43.

25. Butler, "Capacity Utilization and the Rate of Profitability in Manufacturing," p. 239.

26. Kenneth Strand and Thomas Dernburg, "Cyclical Variation in Civilian Labor Force Participation," REVIEW OF ECONOMICS AND STATISTICS, XLVI (November 1964), 387.

27. Ibid., p. 388.

28. See above, this chapter.

29. Nourse, AMERICA'S CAPACITY TO PRODUCE, p. 416.

30. Ibid., p. 406.

31. Ibid., p. 414.

32. Ibid., pp. 416-422.

33. Loeb, REPORT OF THE NATIONAL SURVEY OF POTENTIAL PRODUCT CAPACITY, pp. xxff.

34. Ibid., pp. xxii, 199-200, and 237-238.

35. Leon H. Keyserling, "The Problem of Problems: Economic Growth," in SOCIAL POLICIES FOR AMERICA IN THE SEVENTIES: NINE DIVERGENT VIEWS, edited by Robert Theobald (New York: Doubleday and Company, Inc., 1968), pp. 1-24.

36. Leon H. Keyserling, TWO TOP-PRIORITY PROGRAMS TO REDUCE UNEMPLOYMENT (Washington, D.C.: Conference on Economic Progress, 1963), p. 9.

37. Leon H. Keyserling, TOWARD FULL EMPLOYMENT AND FULL PRODUCTION: HOW TO END OUR NATIONAL ECONOMIC DEFICITS (Washington, D.C.: Conference on Economic Progress, 1954), p. 11n.

38. Ibid., pp. 3 and 6.

39. Leon H. Keyserling, PROGRESS OR POVERTY (Washington, D.C.: Conference on Economic Progress, 1964), p. 99.

40. Leon H. Keyserling, AGRICULTURE AND THE PUBLIC INTEREST: TOWARD A NEW FARM PROGRAM (Washington, D.C.: Conference on Economic Progress, 1965), p. 29.

41. Keyserling, "The Problem of Problems," p. 5.

· 42. U.S. Congress, Senate, Committee on Government Operations, FULL OPPORTUNITY AND SOCIAL ACCOUNTING ACT, HEARINGS, before a subcommittee of the Committee on Government Operations, Senate, on S. 843, Part 2, 90th Cong., 1st sess., 1967, p. 288.

43. Keyserling, "The Problem of Problems," p. 23.

44. Keyserling, PROGRESS OR POVERTY, p. 99.

45. U.S. Congress, Joint Economic Committee, THE POTENTIAL ECONOMIC GROWTH IN THE UNITED STATES, James W. Knowles, Joint Committee Print, Study Paper 20 (Washington, D.C.: Government Printing Office, 1960), pp. 6-7.

46. Ibid., pp. 9, 12, 25, and 35.

47. U.S. Department of Commerce, BUSINESS CONDITIONS DIGEST (Washington, D.C.: Government Printing Office, 1971), 55.

48. Committee for Economic Development, FURTHER WEAPONS AGAINST INFLATION: MEASURES TO SUPPLEMENT GENERAL FISCAL AND MONETARY POLICIES (New York: Committee for Economic Development, 1970), p. 35.

Chapter 7
Estimation of Potential Output and the Economic Surplus

1. Kenneth Strand and Thomas Dernburg, "Cyclical Variation in Civilian Labor Force Participation," REVIEW OF ECONOMICS AND STATISTICS, XLVI (November 1964), 388.

2. Robert F. Martin, NATIONAL INCOME IN THE U.S., 1799-1938 (New York: National Industrial Conference Board, 1939), pp. 6-7.

3. U.S. Department of Commerce, Bureau of the Census, STATISTICAL ABSTRACT OF THE UNITED STATES, 1971 EDITION (Washington, D.C.: Government Printing Office, 1971), p. 306.

4. Ibid., pp. 306-307.

5. U.S. Congress, Joint Economic Committee, THE POTENTIAL ECONOMIC GROWTH IN THE UNITED STATES, by James W. Knowles, Joint Committee Print, Study Paper 20 (Washington, D.C.: Government Printing Office, 1960), p. 40.

Chapter 8
The Economic Surplus and Neo-Marxism:
Comparison and Conclusions

1. Paul A. Baran and Paul M. Sweezy, MONOPOLY CAPITAL: AN ESSAY ON THE AMERICAN ECONOMIC AND SOCIAL ORDER (New York: Monthly Review Press, 1966).

2. Ibid., p. 53.

3. For other ramifications of this view, see Andreas G. Papandreou, PATERNALISTIC CAPITALISM (Minneapolis: University of Minnesota Press, 1972), pp. 80ff.

4. Baran and Sweezy, MONOPOLY CAPITAL, p. 9.

5. Paul A. Baran, THE POLITICAL ECONOMY OF GROWTH (New York: Monthly Review Press, 1957), pp. 23 and 23n.

6. Raymond Lubitz, "Monopoly Capitalism and Neo-Marxism," in CAPITALISM TODAY, edited by Daniel Bell and Irving Kristol (New York: Basic Books, 1970), p. 169.

7. Ibid., p. 170. See also Papandreou, PATERNALISTIC CAPITALISM, p. 43.

8. See David Ricardo, "Principles of Political Economy and Taxation," in CLASSICS OF ECONOMIC THEORY, edited by George W. Wilson (Bloomington, Indiana: Indiana University Press, 1964), p. 243; and Paul M. Sweezy, THE THEORY OF CAPITALIST DEVELOPMENT: PRINCIPLES OF MARXIAN POLITICAL ECONOMY (New York: Monthly Review Press, 1942, 1968), pp. 53ff.

9. Baran and Sweezy, MONOPOLY CAPITAL, pp. 72 and 79.

10. Ibid., pp. 79-81.

11. That is, in later chapters Baran and Sweezy approach the question as to whether enough of this investment-seeking portion can be wasted to avoid stagnation. See ibid., Chapters 5, 6, and 7.

12. Baran and Sweezy, MONOPOLY CAPITAL, pp. 180ff.

13. Ibid., Chapters 5, 6, and 7.

14. Ibid., pp. 161 ff and 213-217.

15. This seeming redundancy of phrase is necessitated by the confusion in the literature between the short run (cyclical) and the long run (secular) motions of capitalism. See, for further discussion and references, Howard J. Sherman, RADICAL POLITICAL ECONOMY: CAPITALISM AND SOCIALISM FROM A MARXIST-HUMANIST PERSPECTIVE (New York: Basic Books, 1972), Chapter 7.

16. The classic statement of this scenario is Thorstein Veblen, THE ENGINEERS AND THE PRICE SYSTEM (Harbinger, ed.; New York: Harcourt Brace and World, 1963). The modern statement is John Kenneth Galbraith, THE NEW INDUSTRIAL STATE (Boston: Houghton-Mifflin Company, 1967). For a

comparison of these two along this line of thought, see J.R. Stanfield, "Veblen's 'Revolutionary Overturn' and THE NEW INDUSTRIAL STATE," REVIEW OF SOCIAL THEORY, I (September 1972), 12-18.

17. Peruse, for example, the new journals, REVIEW OF RADICAL POLITI-CAL ECONOMICS and UPSTART as well as the comprehensive book by Sherman, RADICAL POLITICAL ECONOMY.

18. Sherman, RADICAL POLITICAL ECONOMY, pp. 94-95.

19. Harry G. Johnson, "Economics and Everyday Life" (lecture delivered at the annual banquet of Omicron Delta Epsilon, Oklahoma Alpha Chapter, Norman, Oklahoma, April 21, 1972).

20. Aside from the works of Galbraith and Papandreou referred to often above, two books by Michael Harrington make this point beautifully. See THE ACCIDENTAL CENTURY (Baltimore: Penguin Books, Inc., 1966) and TOWARD A DEMOCRATIC LEFT (Baltimore: Penguin Books, Inc., 1968).

21. Galbraith, THE NEW INDUSTRIAL STATE, especially Chapters 18 to 20.

22. Papandreou, PATERNALISTIC CAPITALISM, pp. 78-80.

23. A.A. Berle, POWER (New York: Harcourt Brace and World, 1967), especially pp. 59-83.

Index

123

About the Author

Ron Stanfield holds the Ph.D. in Economics from the University of Oklahoma, Norman. He is a member of the Union for Radical Political Economics and the Association for Evolutionary Economics. His major research interest is the integration of radical analyses of "monopoly capitalism" with power analyses of the "new industrial state."